PREJUDICE U.S.A.

PREJUDICE
U. S. A.

EDITED BY
CHARLES Y. GLOCK
AND
ELLEN SIEGELMAN

PRAEGER PUBLISHERS
New York • Washington • London

PRAEGER PUBLISHERS
111 Fourth Avenue, New York, N.Y. 10003, U.S.A.
5, Cromwell Place, London S.W.7, England

Published in the United States of America in 1969
by Praeger Publishers, Inc.

Third printing, 1970

Library of Congress Catalog Card Number: 74–75407

Printed in the United States of America

FOREWORD

We Americans are a practical people. We tend to focus on the effects of prejudice, that is, discrimination, rather than on the more mysterious and elusive causes of the problem in men's minds and hearts. This book goes beyond discrimination, and its most virulent representative—racism—to consider what might be done by our social institutions to help eradicate the malevolent attitude we call prejudice.

Unfortunately, no human quality lends itself to self-delusion more than prejudice. We all think we know what it is, and we all absolve ourselves from it. Almost everyone is prejudiced, whether he wants to be or not, and scarcely anyone will admit to it. I am hopeful that, if we could for once truly understand how deeply and subtly evil, how persuasive and omnipresent prejudice is, then we would already be well on the way to curing it. This book leads us in that direction.

My own emphasis in this foreword will be theological and tempered by eleven years of viewing the practical results of prejudice as a charter member of the U.S. Commission on Civil Rights.

Theologically, prejudice has been defined as "rash judgment." Fundamentally, it involves passing detrimental or negative judgment on a person or a group without sufficient

v

evidence. Prejudice brings in its train fear, suspicion, revulsion, hatred—all unfounded and all leading inevitably and irrationally to discrimination, social upheaval, and the denial of human dignity. The excessively generalized hostility encompasses an entire group and becomes the ground for denigrating a single member of the group without reference to his individual merit.

This rash judgment must be distinguished from merely erroneous judgment. It is more pernicious and more inflexible. Shown factual errors behind our other judgments, most of us will modify our views willingly enough. Not so with prejudice. Show a bigot that his negative judgment is falsely founded, and he will quickly find two or three other rationalizations for it in terms of his interests, his values, or imagined or presumed "facts." Prejudice puts out roots in all directions. Destroy one; another is already burgeoning: Demonstrate that Negroes are not biologically inferior, and they may be condemned as lazy for not developing their talents. Prejudice, then, is not only wrong judgment, it is inflexible judgment, almost always finding its outlet in discriminatory action.

Yet, ironically, this poison of personal relations, this corrosive element of our human nature, is not something with which we are born. We learn it; we foster it; and we pass it on to others. It begins because of a perception of difference —difference of color, language, religion, social or economic situation, physical appearance, even sex. We follow this perception of difference with an evaluation and a comparison: What we have or are is the best, so anything different must be inferior. Prejudice has led to and fed on war, oppression, conquest, slavery. One thinks of the hostility between Jew and Arab, Occidental and Oriental, Irishman and Englishman, German and Frenchman, or Northerner and Southerner in a host of countries (Korea, Vietnam, the United States, and many others).

Gordon Allport has given more dignified names to these processes of seeing differences and making invidious comparisons. He calls them categorizing and stereotyping. We naturally categorize our perceptions; then, we readily attribute unfavorable qualities to this or that category: All Jews are sly; all Negroes are shiftless; all Catholics are politically ambitious; all Chinese are cruel; and, of course, all *our* kind—whatever "we" happen to be—are to be preferred over all others, whatever their religion, color, or nationality. The sociologist calls this positive prejudice for one's own group ethnocentrism; the theologian calls it pride.

Each of us, in the words of Charles Lamb, is unconsciously a "bundle of prejudice." We have acquired these prejudices since birth—not from outside enemies, not from Martians, but from our fellow men. We have learned them in our families, our neighborhoods, our schools, even, alas, our churches. No force in our culture systematically opposes them. To divest ourselves and our descendants of prejudice will require a profound cultural change. Ultimately, the change must come from within each of us as an individual. But the agents of such individual change may well be our great social institutions.

The institution I know best is the church. And I regard with some optimism its prospects for prejudice-reduction. The ecumenical movement has helped to foster an understanding of the religious values of others, even though they differ in form or expression from one's own. Moreover, the naïve hope that a single religious group can address itself to vast secular problems of interracial justice and human development has almost disappeared. Today, we all accept the notion that religious groups must join together, and must even join with those who profess no religion, to apply their spiritual strength and power of moral suasion to combat this disease of the judgment that threatens to destroy our society and our civic peace.

I deeply believe that religious prejudice has been and will continue to be reduced in the United States. Ill feeling between large groupings of Catholics and Protestants is diminishing greatly, if not disappearing. The Jewish-Gentile tensions dissolve more slowly, but I find that few people are proud of, or even at ease with, anti-Semitism any more.

This book takes a closer look at the churches' accomplishments and shortcomings in combating prejudice, as well as the attempts of our other major institutions—government, the schools, the mass media, industry and labor. It proposes a number of ways whereby these institutions, working alone and in concert, might become considerably more effective instruments in the struggle against prejudice. I find myself particularly in sympathy with the concluding suggestion of the book, which calls for the establishment of a "National Foundation Against Prejudice and Discrimination." Such a foundation, established as a private agency as the book suggests or, perhaps, as a specially created protected arm of the U.S. Commission on Civil Rights, could go a long way to effect coordination in, and give leadership and inspiration to, let's face it, the long and hard struggle we still face if our country is to be freed of its most virulent social disease—the ancient blight of prejudice.

REV. THEODORE M. HESBURGH, C.S.C.
President, University of Notre Dame
Chairman, U.S. Civil Rights Commission

Notre Dame, Indiana
March, 1969

ACKNOWLEDGMENTS

This book owes a debt to many persons, to a number of organizations, to a research program, and to a symposium.

The symposium is the source of the idea for the book and of a considerable part of its contents. Held in Berkeley, California, in March, 1968, as part of the centennial celebration of the University of California, the symposium, called Patterns of American Prejudice, brought together distinguished representatives of major American social institutions for three days of hard analysis and thinking about the problems of prejudice and its progeny, discrimination. We are grateful to the participants, to the University of California, and to its Survey Research Center, its departments of Political Science, Psychology, and Sociology, and University Extension—the joint sponsors of the symposium, for making the record of the proceedings available for this volume.

The research program to which the book is indebted is the University of California Five Year Study of Anti-Semitism in the United States. Three chapters of the book—those by Seymour M. Lipset, by Rodney Stark and Charles Y. Glock, and by M. Brewster Smith—are based on work carried on as part of this program. The full results of their research will be reported in books currently in preparation. The Survey Research Center of the University of California, under whose auspices the research program is being conducted, has graciously authorized the advance publication of the summary reports, which these chapters contain.

The book's obligation to the University of California and to a number of its constituent units has already been acknowledged. The Rockefeller Foundation's support of the symposium and of the editing of this volume needs also to be recognized, as does the Anti-Defamation League of B'nai B'rith's support of the research program.

Earl Babbie, then Assistant Director of the Survey Research Center; Oscar Cohen, Nathan C. Belth, and Sam Elfert, respectively National Program Director, National Public Relations Director, and Audio-Visual Director of the Anti-Defamation League; and Katherine Devaney of University Extension have furthered the preparation of this book through the important roles they played in the organization and management of the symposium. We are grateful to Mr. Cohen and to Stan Wexler, also of the Anti-Defamation League, for special assistance rendered during the editorial process. Finally, our obligation to the contributors to this volume is unbounded. They were patient, understanding, cooperative, and hard working during the period of our mutual effort.

CHARLES Y. GLOCK
ELLEN SIEGELMAN

November, 1968

CONTENTS

FOREWORD   REV. THEODORE M. HESBURGH   *v*

ACKNOWLEDGMENTS   *ix*

INTRODUCTION   *xiii*

One. Ends and Means in the Struggle for
Equality   SAUNDERS REDDING   *3*

Two. Prejudice and Politics in the American
Past and Present
SEYMOUR MARTIN LIPSET   *17*

Three. Prejudice and the Churches
RODNEY STARK and CHARLES Y. GLOCK   *70*

Four. The Mass Media and Prejudice
DORE SCHARY   *96*

Five. The Schools and Prejudice: Findings
M. BREWSTER SMITH   *112*

Six. The Schools and the Fight Against
Prejudice   CHARLES E. SILBERMAN   *136*

Seven. Prejudice in the Marketplace
HOWARD J. SAMUELS   *150*

Conclusion. Toward the Control of Prejudice and
Discrimination in American Life   *169*

Epilogue. How It Looks from the Center of
the City   RICHARD HATCHER   *184*

ABOUT THE CONTRIBUTORS   *195*

INTRODUCTION

This is a book about prejudice in American life and about strategies to combat it. Such a book ought not to be necessary. For no theme has been sounded more durably and consistently in the nation's history than that of brotherhood. "Love thy neighbor as thyself," "With liberty and justice for all," "With malice toward none and charity for all," "We are all created equal"—these oft-invoked principles presumably testify to a profound national commitment. But despite our dedication to the theory of brotherhood, in practice Americans have been notably intolerant. From the very beginning, racial, religious, and ethnic prejudice has corroded our social machinery.

To be sure, prejudice has taken different forms. Thus, Irish-Americans, Polish-Americans, Italian-Americans were much more often stigmatized in the past than they are today; anti-Semitism, though persistent, appears to be declining; and, in this ecumenical age, Roman Catholics and Protestants seem to be better disposed toward each other. But prejudice takes many guises, and today the suspicions of whites toward blacks and blacks toward whites appear to be on the rise, and the growing Puerto Rican and Mexican-American minorities increasingly feel the pain of ethnic hostility.

While the perpetrators and the victims have changed, intolerance has characterized every generation of Americans, although each generation—including this one—has sought to convince itself that it was more tolerant than its predecessors. Even if prejudice were decreasing, we could not afford to be complacent, for it is abundantly clear, and will be demonstrated again and again in this book, that a substantial minority of Americans are deeply prejudiced and that the vast majority bear some ill will toward other groups.

In the light of American principles, both the existence and the persistence of prejudice are somewhat enigmatic. If prejudice is abhorred, why is it so frequently entertained, and why is there so much complacency about the gap between principle and practice? Are we suffering from massive hypocrisy, or from a kind of national schizophrenia, or what? No one answer will suffice, of course. Perhaps the most cogent explanation is that prejudice is simply not recognized for what it is. While one may readily describe another person as prejudiced, he will almost never apply that epithet to himself. In our society there are few self-proclaimed bigots.

Part of the difficulty in recognizing one's own prejudiced feelings arises because they often spring from irrational beliefs about various racial, religious, or ethnic groups. The bigot also holds certain facts to be correct that are demonstrably not true, for example, the anti-Semite's view that international banking is controlled by Jews. Similarly, he attributes evident differences between groups in status or performance to false causes: for him, it is not socio-economic factors and centuries of oppression that have concentrated Negroes in the lower echelons of society but, rather, something inherent in race itself. And in his response to a despised group, the prejudiced man is prone to generalize excessively, to translate individual truths into general ones, and to magnify slight differences into stereotypic exaggerations.

The bigot's blindness to his own irrationality has the peculiar effect of preventing him from identifying his response as prejudiced. For him, what he believes to be unqualifiedly true and bad about the group reasonably warrants his negative response. On occasion, as is illustrated by the phrase "Some of my best friends . . . ," the bigot may acknowledge exceptions to his rules, but the exceptions only serve to prove the rule and to illustrate his lack of prejudice. The following quotations from respondents to a recent study of prejudice illustrate the mental gymnastics involved:

> The questionnaire is apparently for the use of finding out if I am prejudiced against Negroes or Jews *which I can say I am not*. I feel they should have a place in the community if they earn the right. So far the Negroes are uneducated and unclean and haven't earned their place in the average community. The Jews are neither and they fit in most any place, but they are underhanded and sneaky. [A middle-aged housewife; italics hers.]

> Some of my replies in connection with races and faiths, other than my own, might seem prejudiced to some. But during my forty years of business life I have had a very good opportunity to observe the characteristics of the Negro and the Jew. Granted that some are much better men and women than I am. However, in my opinion, by far more than the majority of them retain the distinctive traits attributed to their race and/or faith. . . . Jews, as a rule, try almost every devious trick in the book to alleviate themselves from the fulfillment of their obligations. [A retired executive.]

In both cases, this kind of thinking is an effective instrument of self-delusion. It eliminates guilt and anxiety about a gap between principle and practice by denying that the gap exists. Once one is convinced that his feelings are warranted, it is unnecessary to think of them as prejudices; hence, the principle of tolerance is left inviolate. One can recite the golden rule and at the same time—without a pang of conscience or any felt dissonance—move away from the neighborhood if a Negro family moves next door.

The absence in American history of any concerted national effort to combat prejudice is largely a result of this process of self-delusion. Most of the prejudiced acknowledge no problem and therefore see no need for reform. The unprejudiced minority have been neither sufficiently powerful nor well organized enough to exert leverage on the national conscience or on those institutions of our society capable of sustaining a massive educational onslaught against prejudice.

So, by necessity and by default, the major task of combating prejudice has fallen to the victims themselves. They are the ones who hurt enough to try to do something. On occasion, they have managed to break through the barriers, to touch the conscience of the majority. It is the victims, more than any others, who have helped sensitize—however slightly —the nation's schools, churches, governments, business, and mass media.

Unfortunately, from the standpoint of cultural pluralism, the successes achieved by the victims appear to correlate directly with their loss of minority identity. Today the Irish, Italians, Germans, Russians, and Poles in the United States have mostly been absorbed into the melting pot, and, as their ethnic identity has disappeared, so have most of the prejudices against them. In turn, the reduction of prejudice makes further assimilation easier.

This ameliorative spiral has not worked for those who would not or could not lose their group identity so readily— that is, for Jews, who have traditionally been a more cohesive social and religious group than some others; and for those, such as Negroes, whose skin color allows for them to be physically differentiated. Prejudice against such minorities has been very stubborn, and whatever success has been achieved in eradicating it has come largely from the group's power to influence legislation and to engage in educational activities on its own behalf. Of course, enlightened non-Jews had some part in spurring the decline of anti-Semitism in the United States. But again, as with other minority groups, Jews themselves have taken the most active role in combating anti-Semitism. Similarly, enlightened whites have helped in the increasing efforts to fight racial prejudice and discrimination. But the success of such efforts—where they have succeeded—has been due to the power and influence of the black community. Other groups—American Indians, Mexican-Americans, Puerto Ricans—have had less done on their behalf so far, but also have not yet acquired the political and economic resources to do more for themselves. There is a basic irony here—the more one needs help, the less likely one is to get it. Oppression is fought effectively, it seems, only when the oppressed are themselves capable of engaging the enemy. One may well ask whether the burden must continue to be carried by the victims primarily, or whether we can become sufficiently mature as a people to engage in a concerted national effort to reduce or eliminate prejudice.

The difficulties of such an effort are obvious, and it is always possible to find excuses, such as "America has survived prejudice before." It *has* survived these divisive attitudes but always at great cost. And now the prospect is that the cost will escalate sharply. Twenty-four million black Americans are no longer willing to abide injustice quietly. Four million Mexican-Americans can be expected to join their ranks as they generate the group solidarity necessary to wage the struggle for their full civil rights. An equally large proportion of Americans may have been victims of prejudice in the past, but never have so many had the will and power to protest loudly and, if peaceful protest fails, violently. As the

Report of the President's Commission on Civil Disorders made clear, the problem of prejudice must be effectively solved. If it is not, we will witness an era of civil strife and internal disorder on the one hand and repressive counter-measures on the other, leading to a polarized, paranoid America consisting of two societies, one white, one black, which only the worst extremist would welcome.

We have been talking all along about prejudice, the root cause of much domestic unrest, and the prime target—under the label of "white racism"—of the Kerner Commission report.[1] But neither the Commission nor anyone else has proposed that the key to solving America's most pressing domestic problem is eliminating prejudice. Rather, the solutions recommended and tried have been addressed almost exclusively to eradicating *discrimination*. Of course, prejudice and discrimination are closely related—the thought is father to the deed. But it is possible to be prejudiced against the members of a group without treating them unfairly: One may dislike Jews and not discriminate against them. Or, while having strong anti-Negro feelings, one may sell one's house to a Negro because the law says one must. While prejudice may exist without discrimination, discrimination rarely occurs without prejudice. To discriminate or to condone or ignore the discriminatory actions of others nearly always implies some degree of generalized ill will.

Discrimination rather than prejudice has been the focus of most current attempts to improve relations between the races. Discrimination has been the target of virtually all the civil rights legislation passed since the Supreme Court school

[1] The Commission report uses the word "racism" rather than "prejudice." It has been decided here and throughout this book to use "prejudice" because of its more generic quality. "Racism" would not be an appropriate term to designate religious or ethnic prejudice. This usage, however, does not imply disagreement with the Commission's designation of white attitudes toward Negroes in this country as largely racist in character.

desegregation decision of 1954, including legislation relating to employment practices, housing, voting, and so on. Why this focus on discrimination rather than on prejudice, the matrix from which discrimination springs? Partly, this course may have been dictated by the victims' priorities—they ask the society to stop hurting them rather than to love them. Further, discrimination is easier to stop. Legislation, the principal means of change available to the state, can help reduce the occasions on which color of skin sets limitations on where one can live, work, play, and learn. And in time, some studies have shown, the very failure to discriminate can lead to changes in attitudes. But in general, of course, one cannot by legislation make friends out of strangers, replace hatred with love, or erase color from the criteria men use to judge each other.

So, simply because discrimination is more subject to control, it has become the natural starting place for a nation obliged to start somewhere. On the positive side, such efforts have been symbolically important and in some areas have helped break down discriminatory barriers. Moreover, all the publicity attending the introduction, passage, and enforcement of civil rights legislation has undoubtedly made some Americans aware of the discrimination the nation has tolerated. Some may even have been moved to look more closely at their own feelings about other groups; while few are prepared to acknowledge their own prejudice, as we have already noted, some may have come to see that the apathy of men of good will (as they no doubt regard themselves) is its own form of prejudice, leading to the tacit acceptance of discrimination.

But any attempt to reduce discrimination without simultaneously trying to change people's attitudes is probably doomed to half-measures, token compliance, and a series of transient victories accompanied by deep resentments. Legislation against discrimination has been difficult to pass, and its enforcement has met widespread and sometimes explosive resistance. Compensatory programs have had trouble getting financed and have been strongly resisted whenever they have affected the *status quo* of the white majority. For the victims of discrimination, great expectations have been generated, but these remain largely unfulfilled. Prejudice on both sides has been exacerbated, making even harder the search for the solutions to the problem of discrimination.

Whether the result might have been different had we made a national effort to combat prejudice is hard to say. Chances are that a program to educate people about the cure and prevention of prejudice begun 'back in 1954 at the time of the Supreme Court decision might by now have borne some fruits. And a program begun now would make it easier for succeeding generations. But even if one agrees that the reduction of prejudice ought to be as much a national goal as the reduction of discrimination, one is immediately struck by overwhelming questions: What should we do? How should we do it? History, common sense, the collective wisdom about human nature and human relations—all these seem to suggest a rather cynical view of the prospects for eliminating prejudice. And yet one cannot help but feel that with enough commitment and ingenuity, a beginning can be made in our age.

The present volume offers no clear-cut or integrated program for disencumbering men of their prejudices. It advances no easy way to show that history or common sense has been wrong. Such a goal is far beyond the purview of any one book. These papers are intended mainly to stimulate thought about the intertwined problems of prejudice and discrimination in America, ultimately to arouse a more widespread concern about the need for the nation to do something about prejudice and something more about discrimination. Only through such concern will we move to make a national effort to destroy the blight that continues to mar the American spiritual landscape.

This book operates under its own assumption—or prejudice, if you will. That is, we believe that the greatest promise for reducing prejudice and discrimination in America lies with the major social institutions. Consequently, the book is devoted to exploring the posture and potential of the nation's schools, churches, mass media, industry and labor, and governmental agencies in the thrust for equality.

The volume begins with an essay by Saunders Redding setting forth the human values to which our society should aspire and the appropriate and legitimate means to reach these goals—both for the white majority and for the nonwhite minority. Dr. Redding's perspective on prejudice, particularly racial prejudice, sets the keynote for the succeeding papers.

This call to conscience is followed by a series of essays examining the inadequacies and the achievements—past, present, and potential—of major American social institutions in the control of prejudice. Seymour Martin Lipset contributes a historical essay on appeals to prejudice by political groups of this country. Rodney Stark and Charles Y. Glock look at prejudice in the church—its leaders and followers, its principle and practice. The mass media's attempts and their unfinished business are examined by Dore Schary.

Prejudice in the schools is the subject of two essays: The first, by M. Brewster Smith, reports the results of a study of prejudice and discrimination among high school students, which serves as a springboard for some generalizations about the school as reinforcer and extinguisher of prejudiced attitudes. The second, by Charles E. Silberman, considers where and why the schools fall short and how they may make up for these shortcomings in education for equality. The final institution assayed is industry, whose role in prejudice reduction is described by Howard J. Samuels.

This serial examination of the major institutions is followed by an integrated overview presented by the editors in the concluding essay of the book. The institutional ideal for prejudice reduction is compared with the previous analyses of the *status quo* in the various institutions, and a strategy is presented for reducing the gap.

The book's epilogue, by Richard Hatcher, echoes and reinforces the themes of the opening essay and of the book as a whole: that prejudice is indeed inimical to the American dream, that this dream must become a reality for all our citizens, that tolerance does not and must not imply tolerance of those who discriminate and those who hate.

In its emphasis the book reflects the special salience of racial prejudice at this time in our national life. Indeed, some authors have focused their contributions almost entirely on racial problems as exemplified by white-black relations. It is hoped that the reader will understand the reasons for this emphasis and will be sensitive to the implications of what is said for the victims of prejudice whatever their race, religion, or national origin.

C.Y.G.
E.S.

PREJUDICE U.S.A.

ONE

ENDS AND MEANS IN THE STRUGGLE FOR EQUALITY

SAUNDERS REDDING

It is dangerously easy to oversimplify the change in the psychological dynamics of the racial situation in America during the past decade. True, public consciousness has changed somewhat, and a small but vocal segment of concerned citizens is beginning to evaluate racial problems in human terms. We see the evidence of this concern in the difference between such humane documents as the 1965 Moynihan report and the Kerner Commission report on the one hand and the drily official studies of race relations sponsored by Congress in 1919, 1928, and 1945 on the other.

But the "new" black of whom we have been hearing lately --self-assertive, self-confident, militant, determined—is not so new. Perhaps one might say that his tactics are new, but his goals have not changed. Negroes have always sought to secure their elementary rights. Ignored though it has been by some of our most distinguished historians, evidence of the Negro's preoccupation with freedom and equality is abundant. In the century since emancipation, black Americans have persistently sought to exercise the civil rights that the Thirteenth, Fourteenth, and Fifteenth amendments were designed to guarantee. Indeed, it was the very fear of Negro success that solidified white attitudes in the South and

3

spawned a profusion of laws and extralegal devices designed to subvert these amendments and force the black man's accommodation to the social, political, and economic system that denied him his rights.

Though the struggle in which the black man is presently engaged is not new, there are some new elements in the general situation—particularly the public awareness of his struggle. The 1954 decision of the U.S. Supreme Court marked a change in the official reaction to that struggle. The judicial branch of the federal government affirmed in simple, understandable language that the "separate but equal" rationalization, which perpetuated the inferior status of the black man, was no longer to be honored. In this and subsequent decisions, the Supreme Court helped to translate the needs of Negroes—long continued but long ignored—into the stated policy of government.

The 1954 decision also generated a more intense resurgence of the struggle of Negroes for justice and equality. It is no coincidence that the Montgomery bus boycott occurred within the next two years, followed shortly afterward by the sit-ins, the freedom rides, and all the other dramatic indications of the black man's insistence that his rights as an American citizen be respected. The initial success of his tactics justified and reinforced his confidence in the "American way" and brought about further change in the patterns of race relations.

But since these early achievements, and especially during the last few years, pessimism about progress in civil rights has been growing. This pessimism can be explained in terms of a set of forces noted by the distinguished psychologist Kenneth Clark, who wrote that

The central problems posed in attempting to understand what is happening to the Negro and in America are the problems of the rapidity of change (complicated by the unevenness of change) and the effects of old patterns of accommodation on the part of both whites and Negroes in their ability to adjust to the new realities.[1]

It is within this context that one must seek to understand what has happened. First, the problem of change: In pragmatic terms, we *have* had change, and it has been swifter than scarcely anybody thought possible, faster than the white majority deemed either necessary or wholesome. As the Negro moved from rural and southern areas into more sophisticated urban areas, formal discrimination appeared to decrease. In fields such as health, employment, individual incomes, and voter registration, statistics show large percentage gains for black Americans over the last twenty years. Indeed, these gains are often larger than the corresponding percentage gains for whites. But these statistics leave out more than they tell, for the starting level for Negroes in all these areas was so low that even with improvement, their status remains far below that of whites. For example, although family incomes for Negroes went up 73 per cent in the year 1959–60, median Negro family income was still only about half that of whites, and although the percentage of Negroes in college doubled from 1940 to 1960, it too was only about half that of whites.

Black Americans compare themselves not with where they were twenty years ago but with where white Americans are today. As Thomas Pettigrew, the social psychologist, put it:

> The Negro is . . . considerably more frustrated today than he was at the beginning of this period of change because, while his absolute standard has been going up, his aspiration level has been rising much faster. His relative deprivation, the difference between what he has and what he thinks is his right to

[1] Kenneth B. Clark, *Dark Ghetto* (New York, Harper & Row, 1965).

have, is now probably greater than at any other time in American history.[2]

While charging that relative deprivation is probably the primary dynamic in the black protest movement today, Pettigrew was echoing the judgment of many that the Negro is on a treadmill and actually stands to lose ground, relatively speaking, in the years ahead.

The change that has occurred has not only been small relative to needs, it has been uneven. Thus, the rapid desegregation of some places of public accommodation and recreation, bus lines, and libraries, has been accompanied by a damnably slow desegregation of public schools, by "tokenism" on many fronts, and by the average American's desire to avoid controversy and violence, to close his eyes to problems—without regard to the moral costs.

The Legacy of Crippling Patterns

The other factor in this equation of conflict noted by Professor Clark is the persistence of old patterns that have damaged both races and corroded the human spirit of one no less than the other. Our segregated society has depressed motivation, generated conflicts in self-esteem, and restricted the perspectives of Negroes. It has also created in the white man an exaggeration of the importance of his whiteness—entirely apart from capacities and attainments. In the South, particularly, the segregated society blinded him to the insidious moral and social consequences of the race-caste system and led him to equate force with authority and his way of life with the good life. One thinks of the obvious instances—

2 Thomas Pettigrew, "White-Negro Confrontations," in *The Negro Challenge to the Business Community,* edited by Eli Ginzberg (New York: McGraw-Hill, 1964).

Senator James O. Eastland, Jim Clark, George Wallace, and "Bull" Connor—but evidence gathered by social scientists seems to support the conclusion that no man, white or black, socialized in America in the past century, could escape the influences of racism which permeates every aspect of American life.

Therefore, even as we attempt to abolish discrimination and segregation, we must find ways to deal with the continuing social and psychological effect of past discrimination. It will be a long time yet before we no longer hear the questions "Yes, but would you want a Negro for a neighbor?" and "Would you want your daughter to marry a Negro?" and perhaps an even longer time before the Negro gets over his distrust of white faces. Neither the complex dynamics of group self-adulation among whites nor of group self-hatred among Negroes will be dissipated or rendered inoperative by law. The passage of a law will not at one stroke modify the white man's beliefs about himself and his legacy of myths about race; nor will the operation of a law at once free the Negro from his heritage of self-rejection and dependence. Present proof is to be found in the extreme difficulty that moderate and even some liberal whites have in accepting the "all-or-none" principle of integration and in their persistent advice to Negroes to pace out their demands. On the other side, the proof is found in the appeal of the Black Muslims' idea of a Negro uniracial state. And on both sides, there are practical consequences.

Eventually, the operation of the law, by forcing changes in behavior, will change attitudes. We have had evidence from a number of studies that under favorable conditions such compliance does foster a positive change in attitude. But meanwhile the mere absence of discrimination and segregation will not bring about the equality of black people, nor will it appreciably change the dreary statistics of their functional inferiority so often cited by so many and used as arguments against integration. They have been disadvantaged for 300 years, and the fact of it shows in all the indices of education, economics, and social behavior. They have been badly educated or not educated at all; underemployed or not employed at all. Many have been driven to apathy or to antisocial behavior. Overcoming these handicaps to assimilation, linked as they are to disadvantaged status, will not be easy. Unless we act on the proposition that the implementation of the rights of citizenship can be accomplished only through equalizing opportunity and the base from which that opportunity can be exploited, the handicaps will not be overcome at all.

This diagnosis of the prevalence of patterns of injustice and of their corroding effects brings us to two major prescriptions. One of these is addressed primarily to the white majority. This has to do with a recognition that abolition of discrimination—the granting of legal equality based on presumed present equality of opportunity—is not enough. Whites must be prepared to recognize the just necessity for compensatory treatment (of this, more later).

The other major prescription has to do with the tactics Negroes and other minorities must adopt to teach themselves and the white majority what their demands are and how to secure those rights. Both these strategies must be pursued simultaneously, and both make demands for fairness in considering the needs of all the people, not just white people or black people.

One Road to Equality:
Minority Solidarity and Cultural Pluralism

First let us look at the minority strategy. It is common to refer to the present civil rights struggle as a revolution and to think of it as seeking change through a "sudden break with the past." The spirit of a revolution is "not tomorrow, but now; not part of the way, but all the way." But all the way to what? There is nothing automatic about the outcome of a revolution. Revolutions must be planned and managed; their leaders must constantly evaluate what it takes to win. The unique thing about the present civil rights revolution is that its general purpose has not been to overthrow the basic structure of society. Its purpose has been only to move the black man from outside the social structure to a place within it. Basically, and in spite of the yammering of black extremists, the Negro wants no one put out—he simply wants in. There can be no doubt that this desire for inclusion is complicated by other factors, such as the existence of ghettos and slum housing, the problems of poverty in the midst of affluence, the archaic forms of local government and the way it works, substandard education, and increasing automation and cybernation. But if we are to maintain the political and moral values of our country, these problems too must be solved.

So far, however, they have not yielded to protest. Protest tends to produce a grudging token compliance, and tokenism is a sign that revolutionary ends have been stymied and that the walls of exclusion have been shored up. There is no such thing as instant revolution. Revolution, as Hannah Arendt points out, comprises a before and an after. And this revolution has not completed the "before" yet. In order to complete it, other strategies must be devised. In some ways the climate is favorable. For poor as the blacks' education is as compared to that of whites, it is much better now than it ever has been. Today our minorities are more aware of their rights and of the great gulf between their status and that envisioned for all citizens in the law of the land. Today, also, more people realize that the unresolved race problem weighs against the nation's effort to maintain its leadership in the world.

Though all these factors suggest that the climate for change is favorable, there remains considerable cause for concern. There is the painful conflict in Vietnam. There is an increasingly tough resistance on the part of the white supremacists; and, as in the Reconstruction era of nearly 100 years ago, an alliance of white supremacists and political opportunists can defeat the economically and politically powerless, the ignorant and the naïve. Recent events offer some evidence of a return to violence as a means of keeping the minority-group member in his place. Moreover, too many people, even among the well-meaning, see the minority condition as self-imposed. If the dark-skinned American really wants to improve his condition, these people say, it is up to him. If he has fewer opportunities and fewer rewards, he has only himself to blame. His failure is an individual failure and has nothing to do with racial status. Let him work harder, save his money, fix up his property, behave less conspicuously, acquire cultural interests congruent with those of the community at large, and his problems will disappear. It will be only a matter of time. Look at the Jews, the Irish, the Poles, the Italians—haven't they solved their problems in this way?

But this approach cannot begin to solve the problem. It is based on the premise that members of a cultural subgroup gradually lose those characteristics that set them apart from the majority and thus become indistinguishable from that group. But by the very fact of their color, the Negro, the Indian, the Mexican-American cannot meet that condition. The "melting-pot" approach is based upon the supposition that if someone from a minority group attains the highest point in personal and professional accomplishment and financial security, group subordination and exploitation can no longer touch him. One has only to look at the abuses suffered by Ralph Bunche, Percy Julian, Marion Anderson, or Willie Mays to realize how false this supposition is.

If racial minorities cannot defend themselves by submerging their identities and becoming indistinguishable from the majority group, what can they do instead? They can learn—and, in fact, they seem to be learning—to protect themselves by creating conflict in the white man's field of interest—between, let us say, his socially exploitative behavior on the one hand and his bank balance on the other. The essential requirement for doing this is group solidarity. Yet despite some evidence to the contrary, group solidarity has been largely missing in the present struggle. It has been missing partly because it inevitably raises the question of group identity, and it is group identity that created the race problem in the first place. The fact that group identity can here be justified as a necessary means to a desirable end does not lessen the skepticism with which so many view it. They are caught between the American ideal of individualism and the pragmatic knowledge that this ideal does not seem to have much meaning for the individual who is black, or brown, or red.

Until black Americans give greater value to group identity, their power can never be mobilized to the end of equalizing the individual Negro's life chances. Every Negro institution, beginning with the family, must place high value on cooperation for group goals, while at the same time continuing to promote individual initiative and accomplishment. The pattern must be visible throughout the civil rights structure. It should not be limited to a public show of togetherness. On the part of civil rights leaders, there must be a deep commitment to mutual aid. They must determine together the primary areas of policy concern, but at the same time they must recognize that to a growing degree, policy and programs will not be geared to Negro civil rights and racial equality alone. Increasingly, one hopes, the issues they face will relate to the social, economic, cultural, and political development of the whole community. The Negro leaders' job will be to see to it that the policies and programs on local, state, and national levels do not work to the detriment or only to the minimum benefit of the black man. *Black identity must be fostered with the aim of joining racial goals to the goals of other minority groups and of other interest groups, such as labor and industry, trade and commerce, religion and politics.*

In other words, I advocate a cultural pluralism within which black institutions, including the family, would preserve their distinctive qualities and interact with other institutions to keep viable the distinctly American idea of "equality in difference." But I also advocate individual integration and assimilation, in which it would be recognized that man—any man of any color or creed—was free to lose or to maintain his group identity as he chose. I advocate a pattern of life and a way of thinking in which it would be recognized and respected that a man has free access to all the rights, responsibilities, and duties that inhere in the American system— that he marry white or black at his own discretion, and without penalties imposed on the basis of his color; that he live wherever he choose and on any standard he can afford. In short, I advocate equality. But the equality must first be attained. And this thought takes me back to the beginning and brings me near the end of this paper.

Another Road to Equality:
Compensatory Treatment for the Mistreated

At the same time that the black community is using its group solidarity to confront whites in areas of their self-interest, the white community must also open avenues to equality. It must act on the notion that the years of mistreatment require massive compensatory effort. Only in this way will the balance be restored and equality of opportunity—actual, not just legal—be guaranteed.

When Whitney Young, Executive Director of the National Urban League, first put forth the concept of favored treatment for Negroes, in 1966, a roar of disapproval went up from whites and even from a handful of blacks who thought that he was premature in his talk about preferential or compensatory treatment. Whether or not this recommendation was premature, we must be concerned with this concept and with the will of white Americans to accept it. There are a great many white people opposed to it. They say that preferential treatment is discrimination in reverse. They say that it is no fairer for blacks to ask for favored treatment over whites than it is for whites to get favored treatment over blacks.

There are those who say justice demands equality but without regard to color, and special treatment for blacks means recognizing color at the very time when history seems to be moving toward the obliteration of color in the dispensing of justice. Black people are not different from other minorities, they say, so why should they demand something no other minority has ever demanded? Certainly, they say, we cannot be asked to give support to a concept that will favor them at our expense. The demand for it is hypocritical, selfish, ignorant, and immoral.

Now this would seem a valid argument on its face—especially in the light of the belief that in a democracy everybody has an equal opportunity. But the argument leaves out too much. It leaves out particularly an issue that should have some weight. We know now that slavery was a social evil, and more of us are coming to believe that segregation and discrimination are also social evils. So the question is whether America owes a moral debt to black citizens for the wrongs they have admittedly suffered through no fault of their own. The simple, true answer would seem to be yes. Yet, as I have said, there is the cry of discrimination in reverse. Many do not like the term "compensatory treatment" any better than "favored" or "preferential treatment." In fact, they like it much less. It focuses too directly on 300 years of the mistreatment of blacks at the hands of whites. But it was certainly compensation that Whitney Young had in mind, and I believe he spoke for the majority of his race.

Compensatory treatment for the disadvantaged is logically sound, socially just. There are legal precedents for this principle of compensating the needy and defenseless: child labor laws, the interdiction of sweat shops, the minimum wage bill, social security, Medicare. The doctrine of preferential/ compensatory treatment underlies our national relief programs, aid to education, and the war on poverty. Behind the doctrine lies the belief that the people who benefit from this corrective legislation have been disadvantaged through no fault of their own. The GI Bill, a striking example, was intended to enable veterans to "catch up" with citizens who had not been disadvantaged by military service.

The End in View: An Inclusive American Community

Just as many Negroes infer from their experience that whites are their natural enemies, many whites conclude that Negroes do not share their values, their interests, or their cultural heritage. Both beliefs are weakened by current events. The general insistence on the basic qualities and equalities of citizenship cuts across racial lines. It is part of a nationwide movement, in part government-sponsored now, but almost wholly black in its origins, and it affirms those very humanistic values and interests that the Negro is said not to share. Basically, it is a demand for the elimination of any category defined as intrinsically inferior. It is a demand for the elimination of status-inferiority as such, and if this isn't beating the drums for peculiarly American values, I do not know what is. The civil rights movement is an American movement, and for this reason it has caught up millions of people of widely varying social commitments. It has drawn all faiths of the community—Protestants, Catholics, and Jews—into its vortex. The basic values applied to the concept of the inclusive American community are the sources of the movement's strength.

But let me emphasize the "inclusive American community," for the only solution to the problems of race is the formation of a single community with full membership for all. Resistance to this solution is strong. It shows itself in the current effort of certain political conservatives to ignore the conclusions of the Kerner Commission report and to create a third party on the basis of states' rights and opposition to desegregation. Our society cannot have it both ways. A multiracial democratic society jeopardizes its existence when one of its component groups is denied full access to the society. This is not to say that ethnic and cultural pluralism should not continue and that it cannot make positive contributions to the inclusive American community. But identity in this respect should not imply discrimination. Inclusion must not be qualified by any of the factors—race, religion, national origin —that have hitherto made for exclusion and perverted both the spirit and the letter of American law.

I conclude by reiterating that black Americans are American. In spite of the Black Muslims and the ambivalent appeal of their emotional identification with Muslim Africa, the Negro American is no more African than the fairest Anglo-

Saxon Protestant is. He is American. His destiny is one with the destiny of America. His culture is the culture of Americans, and so are his vices and virtues and problems. Let us not deceive ourselves. In the words of the comic strip character Pogo, "We have seen the enemy, and they is us."

PREJUDICE AND POLITICS IN THE AMERICAN PAST AND PRESENT

SEYMOUR MARTIN LIPSET

The social tensions inherent in rapid economic growth, urbanization, immigration, migration, and shifts in the position of different ethnic groups, have repeatedly in American history stimulated the phenomenon of the political "backlash." Various groups have experienced such changes as challenges to their status, values, or interests; they have reacted by seeking to eliminate the source of these threats, which they have often located in the supposed control over the government, or the institutions that dominate communications and culture, by an immoral, corrupt, and un-American minority, whose covert power has made the formal democratic process meaningless. Extremist movements—such as the anti-Masonic party of the late 1820's, the various nativist and Know-Nothing anti-Catholic parties and orders of the pre–Civil War era, the American Protective Association of the 1890's, the Ku Klux Klan of the 1920's, the Coughlinite movement of the 1930's, the McCarthyite syndrome of the 1950's, and most recently the George Wallace movement in the 1960's—have each in different ways given expression to the sense of frustration of millions of Americans at a threat to their power and status or to their economic position.

This paper will give a brief history of this backlash politics, which is the politics of prejudice whether directed against an oppressed minority group, such as Catholics, Jews, or Negroes, or against a favored minority group, such as an urban elite. In either case, as we shall see, prejudicial appeals are directed against a minority, about whom a theory of conspiracy is invoked as a justification for such prejudice. The use of ethnic, racial, and religious appeals against the supposed threat of minority groups is clearly almost as old as the American political system itself. The efforts of nearly every minority group in the United States to improve its situation have been viewed as a threat by some who possessed dominant status-characteristics, and some political leaders at almost every period have appealed to'such resentments to get votes.

From Prejudicial Appeals to Political Movements

How do such extremist appeals become crystallized into a political movement or a political party? Working on the model proposed by Neil Smelser,[1] we can postulate the following: there must first be a social strain or decline in status which is somewhat ambiguous and creates widespread anxiety. The adherents of extremist movements have typically felt deprived—either they have never gained their due share or they are losing their portion of power and status. We might call these two groups the "never-hads" and the "once-hads." These deprived groups are not necessarily extremist, but extremism usually draws its strength from them. Among the deprived, the first type (never-hads) tends to experience primarily economic deprivation and consequently to seek redress by state action to achieve economic reforms; this type has usually supported left-wing extremism, although it has occasionally fostered right-wing movements as well. The second

---

[1] References are given in the Appendix at the end of this book.

type (once-hads) experiences or fears loss of status and influence; this group cannot be assuaged by government action. It requires a different course of action—usually projecting of grievances onto a minority group and attempting to discredit or destroy that group to relieve its own sense of anxiety; this course of action typically takes the form of right-wing extremism, and it is with such extremism that we will be concerned in our focus on prejudice.

Such reactions are not simply a response to political changes and demands. The fluidity of the American social structure—the fact that no dominant group has ever enjoyed a socially recognized claim to long-term status in the style of some of the more class-ridden societies of the old world—has meant that status insecurity has been an enduring characteristic of American life. New regions, new industries, new migrant groups, new ethnic and religious groups, have continually encroached upon the old. These changes have often been accompanied by adjustments in the prevailing norms concerning proper relations between parents and children, the drinking of alcoholic beverages, the use of drugs, the relations between the sexes, styles of dress, conceptions of religious morality, etc. Such changes in morality lead those adhering to the old norms to feel disinherited, dispossessed, displaced in their own land.

Groups that have a claim to status and cultural influence as a result of past or present achievements turn against existing political institutions when they feel that their claim is insecure, is under attack, or is actually declining. Such groups may include, under present conditions, some among the quite privileged, such as doctors or heads of family-owned corporations who feel the weight of growing government controls; or, on a less affluent level, working-class whites who after gaining economic security feel the pressure of Negro demands on their schools, neighborhoods, and unions; or, on an ideological axis, those whose self-identity is closely linked to traditional religious and secular values that appear to be in the process of being supplanted by concepts and behavior which they view as immoral. These are the protypal situations that have fed the wellsprings of right-wing movements and, indeed, of right-wing extremism.

How do these groups whose status and values are threatened react to such insecurity? As Smelser suggests, they deal with it by designating a specific cause for that strain—not necessarily or typically the real cause, but a plausible cause. In many cases, ethnically or religiously identifiable groups have served that purpose well. The heavy immigration by ethnic groups who have introduced allegedly "un-Protestant" and "un-American" values and modes of behavior into this society has often been identified by "displaced" strata as the main threat to their values or position. So, for example, economic unrest has engendered mass anti-immigrant and anti-Catholic movements among the less privileged classes based on the charges that "alien" competition for jobs was the cause of unemployment. And loss of elections, the growth of urban machine politics, and changes in the general state of social morality commonly have been interpreted by groups losing their economic, social, political, or religious dominance as the fault of foreigners and non-Protestants who have undermined the traditional structure of status and authority. Because nativism has so openly traded on religious and ethnic appeals, it has been of primary importance in determining the correlations between party choice and membership in specific religious and ethnic groups. In most instances in this country, the values that the declining majority has tried to preserve against the rising minorities have been the values of nativism, fundamentalism, and simplistic moralism.

Such moralism—operating as it does largely among the less educated, more fundamentalist, and more provincial—requires the belief that the minority target group is conspiring to destroy the very values that the deprived group is seeking to preserve. Conspiracy theories uniformly describe a high-powered core of intellectuals involved in devious manipulation of the national mind. As we shall see, conspiracy theories have provided the central drive for bigoted American political movements, because they suggest the course of direct action the deprived group must take: the remedy against the alleged conspiratorial plotting of a secret band of intellectuals at the helm of a distrusted minority group is exposure, repression, and even annihilation. And this course of action is presumably justified by the tenets of morality. The moralism of bigotry tends to be absolutist—the enemy is identified with the circulation of corrupt literature and with general debauchery. This black-and-white view insists that the enemy is debarred by its moral corruption and conspiratorial tactics from having any legitimate place in the normative political marketplace. This entire process of backlash politics has characterized segments of American conservatism for much of our country's history.

Early Movements Against the Illuminati, the Masons, and the Catholics

The first such example involved New England Federalists, Congregationalists, and merchants, who reacted to their decline by discovering foreign-based conspiracies and by emphasizing religion and moralism. In the last years of the eighteenth century, they placed the blame for the changing moral order, and their concomitant loss of political power, religious influence, and status, on the conspiratorial activities of the Illuminati. The Illuminati were an Enlightenment society of intellectuals, affiliated to the Masons, that existed for a brief period in Bavaria. Some European writers credited the group with responsibility for the French Revolution and other upheavals in various countries. The anti-Illuminati agitation involved an effort to defeat the rapidly growing Jeffersonian and deist challenges to the position and values of the Congregationalist and Federalist elites by identifying these opponents as agents of a revolutionary conspiracy.

A quarter of a century later, a new wave of exposés of Masonic, and to some extent Illuminati, conspiracies arose during a comparable period in which conservative political and traditional religious forces felt themselves under attack from the rising Jacksonian democracy and irreligious elements. The politically potent anti-Masonic movement drew much of its extensive support from lowly educated poor segments of the rural population which lived away from urban settlements, but it ultimately joined forces with the conservative National Republicans to form the Whig Party. Both waves of agitation against Illuminati-Masonic conspiracies involved ethnic and religious bigotry. The Illuminati of 1798 were identified with the revolutionary activities of the Irish in Ireland and America, while the anti-Masonic party at times espoused nativist, anti-Catholic, and even anti-Semitic sentiments.

Such efforts to identify threats to the religious order and status system with hidden conspiracies, as well as the repeated espousal of anti-Catholic nativism, first by the Federalists and later by the Whigs and related groups in the two decades before the Civil War, illustrate, as we shall see, the willingness of segments of the American elite to encourage extremism in their attempts to hold power. Among the masses, the rise of such movements has frequently represented the responses of evangelical Protestants to the changes that they feared were eroding their moral values or social status.

From the early days of the republic down to the Great Depression, the most important source of prejudice in American politics was anti-Catholicism. Such sentiments have deep religious roots in this country: the Puritans, the Methodists and the Baptists who came to dominate in terms of numbers, all hated the Papists. And this deep streak of anti-Catholic feeling was seized on at different times in American history to sustain movements that sought to preserve existing institutions against the threat of change—a threat that was attributed to the increased number of Catholics in the country and even to conspiracies directed by Rome.

Perhaps the earliest sustained anti-Catholic political effort occurred in New York in the first decade of the nineteenth century. The recently defeated Federalist Party, in an effort to regain strength by appealing to voters' religious prejudice, re-formed as the anti-Catholic American Party,[2] thus initiating the oft-repeated pattern of conservatives resorting to appeals to racial or religious bigotry when they find their power declining.

Anti-Catholicism of the Mid-Nineteenth Century; the Know-Nothings

Anti-Catholicism made its first independent political impact during the 1830's, coinciding with the increase of immigration and with the rise of Jacksonian democracy. During this time, a growing anti-Catholic literature reported the alleged sins and evil designs of the Catholic Church, including revelations of secret sexual activities that presumably went on in convents and monasteries (*Six Months in a Convent, The Nun,* etc.). The Catholics were described as seeking to conquer and corrupt America through sheer numbers— the inpouring of masses of Irish and other immigrants. Scat-

[2] This group was the first to introduce the name "American Party." Some version of the term "American Party" has been used by racists and bigots for well over a century and a half.

tered anti-Catholic parties appeared in eastern cities in the 1830's and grew in numbers and influence in the 1840's.

To a considerable degree the success of this wave of anti-Catholic hysteria seems to be linked to the weakness in the cities in the 1830's and 1840's of the principal conservative party, the Whigs, With the mass base given to the Democrats by the Jacksonian populist image, the Whigs found it increasingly difficult to win elections. They began to blame their defeats at the polls on the fact that foreigners and Catholics were voting overwhelmingly for the Democrats. As more and more foreigners, particularly Catholics, came into the country, many Whigs feared they would be unable to compete effectively with their political rivals. This fear forced them on a number of occasions, from the early 1840's on, to compromise with their presumed dislike of appealing to prejudice by allying themselves with the more aggressively anti-Papist forces organized in the various small parties extolling an America-for-Americans nativism.

The use of anti-Catholicism by the Whigs played on a number of basic Protestant fears and values in an attempt to wean Protestants away from the Democrats. Orthodox Protestants saw in the growing number of Catholics and their increased political influence in the cities a threat to Protestant cultural dominance. The growing number of immigrants, Catholics and others, was regarded as a competitive economic and status threat by many Protestant workers. Furthermore, during this period of rapid population growth and geographic mobility, many Protestants moved from rural to urban areas, and in doing so severed their close social ties to the people and the institutions among which they were reared: they naturally feared the new ways of the city. The Protestants also feared the outcome of Catholic attempts to oppose Protestant teaching and the reading of the Protestant Bible in the public schools. (The Catholics were supported in this demand by religious liberals, deists, and atheists, mainly united in the Democratic party.)

Exploiting all these fears of economic, cultural, and moral displacement, the elaborately ritualistic anti-Catholic secret orders were able to recruit large numbers of Protestants, especially the poor and uneducated, to defend the old values and traditions. The literature that emerged in this period was not only generally anti-Catholic but articulated a specific theory of Catholic conspiracy stemming from Rome, supposedly launched to undermine the American system. Belief in this theory presumably justified violent and undemocratic means to eradicate the conspiracy. From the 1840's to the mid-1850's, violent anti-Catholic riots occurred. Churches and convents were burned and Catholics were beaten. Meanwhile, the Catholics were blamed for urban crime and the growth in immorality.

Given the rationale of moral absolutism, many of the same invidious things that are written openly or said privately about Negroes today were stated about other visible minority groups (primarily Catholic immigrants) at various periods before the Civil War. The themes of crime in the streets, immorality and unfitness, and conspiracy have been staples in the American diet of intolerance.

This rising tide of anti-Catholicism culminated in the emergence of the American, or Know-Nothing, Party in 1854. The latter became for a brief period the second largest party in the United States, since the Whigs generally ceased to run candidates. It captured the government in many Eastern cities as well as Baltimore and New Orleans. Its representatives constituted two-thirds of the Massachusetts legislature and a majority in the Connecticut legislature. In fact, the Know-Nothing Party had political hegemony in most of New England and in many of the Middle Atlantic states.

The political conditions that fostered the rapid growth of

the Know-Nothing Party closely resembled those linked to the spread of the anti-Illuminati agitation in the late 1790's and of the anti-Masonic party at the end of the 1820's. The rise to prominence of these anticonspiratorial movements seems to have been a reaction to the breakdown of the principal conservative political forces of each period. The anti-Illuminati frenzy coincided with the decline of Federalism under John Adams; the anti-Masons arose with the defeat of his equally conservative son John Quincy Adams and the rise of Jacksonian democracy; and the emergence of the Know-Nothings as a mass movement occurred after the breakup of the Whig Party following its defeat in the election of 1852.

Although most American Party votes clearly came from former Whig supporters, the new party was able to win in traditional Democratic areas, particularly in cities, by capturing the backing of many Protestant workers who had previously voted Democratic. In some communities, it even took on a leftist or populist aura on various social issues.

But the Know-Nothings had a relatively short political career. The party broke up by 1857 before it could do much about Catholics or immigrants. It was torn asunder by the slavery issue, which was far more crucial for many devout Protestants than was the anti-Catholic cause. The Northern supporters of the Know-Nothings were devoutly antislavery, while its Southern supporters were equally committed to slavery. A party divided on so crucial an issue could not easily maintain itself.

In the North, the Know-Nothings were absorbed into the new party that expressed the feeling of the middle-class, Protestant, formerly Whig community—the Republicans. The Republican Party, after the Civil War, was to take over the role of the Know-Nothings as the anti-Catholic party. Ulysses S. Grant had been a Know-Nothing for a brief period. As commander of the Union Army during the Civil War,

Grant had tried to bar Jews from areas he controlled. As a Republican President, he made overtly anti-Catholic public statements. In addressing a reunion of Union veterans, he spoke out about the threat of a new civil war between the supporters of superstition (that is, the Catholics) and the true believers; he intimated that the Union Army might have to be recalled to defend the country against the conspiracies of the forces of superstition. Both of Grant's Vice-Presidents had been Know-Nothing leaders before the Civil War. Other Republican presidents and candidates, like Rutherford Hayes and James G. Blaine, were also active in the anti-Catholic fight. On the local level, in the cities, the role of the Republicans as an anti-Catholic party was even more obvious. The statement which supposedly defeated Blaine in the Presidential election of 1884 was the Reverend Blanchard's accusation that the Democrats were "the party of rum, Romanism, and rebellion." Many historians have been so unaware of the role of religion as a perennial source of post-Civil War partisan controversy that this one slogan was mentioned for a long time as having had a decisive effect on the election's outcome. Yet this single allegation could hardly have defeated Blaine, for thousands of Republicans had said the same or worse. Blanchard could legitimately be regarded as having merely epitomized what many Republicans were saying all along.

Two efforts to re-create a party called the American Party during this period failed. The first, which ran Presidential candidates in 1876 and 1880, represented a minor effort by provincial Protestant fundamentalists to revive an anti-Masonic movement, with tinges of anti-Catholicism. Some of the literature of this movement linked radical activities of the day, such as the Paris Commune of 1871 and the American strike wave of the 1870's, with the continued activities of the Illuminati, previously credited with having organized the

French Revolutions of 1789 and 1830. The second American Party of the post-Civil War era was formed in the late 1880's and was primarily anti-Catholic and nativist. Although it tried to mount a national campaign, it, too, found little support for a third party.

The APA and the Populists Around the Turn of the Century

Such efforts to form a new party based on Protestant fears of conspiracy failed, but conditions had changed sufficiently by the end of the 1880's to facilitate the growth of a militantly anti-Catholic movement in the form of the American Protective Association (APA), which was founded in 1887.

At its high point in 1893, the APA and its allied organizations were credited with a membership of about 2 million people. In approach, the APA echoed the Know-Nothings. It repeated many of the Know-Nothing tales of Catholic conspiracy, warned Americans that the Catholics were arming to seize power and kill off Protestants, and accused the Catholics of having assassinated Presidents Lincoln and Garfield. So intense was the anti-Catholic feeling, and so widely held was the conspiracy theory, that a responsible public official, the governor of Ohio, in 1893 issued arms to Protestants to defend themselves against the alleged Catholic plan to kill them. The APA at the time was buying rifles and drilling troops because of its belief that on a specific day the Catholics were going to shoot the Protestants in a manner reminiscent of the St. Bartholomew's Day Massacre in sixteenth-century France. Hundreds of thousands—perhaps millions—of Protestants took this allegation so seriously that they felt they must bear arms to defend themselves against the threat from the Catholic minority. The proportion of Catholics was then not more than that of Negroes now—about 15 per cent; the fear that 15 per cent of the population was going to shoot down and wipe out 85 per cent offers eerie parallels with the contemporary situation.

This dramatic rise of the APA in the early 1890's, like that of the Know-Nothings in the 1850's, seems to have been related to a visible threat to the political domination of the major source of evangelical Protestant control—in this case, the Republican Party. In the Congressional elections of 1890, the Republicans suffered their greatest defeat since their formation, shifting from a House majority to a minority of 88 members as compared to 235 Democrats and 9 Populists. In 1892, the Democrats won the Presidency with their first decisive plurality since 1856. They also held political control of many cities, in which Irish Catholics were beginning to take over as mayors and political leaders. Issues concerning teaching in the public schools continued to divide Protestants and Catholics. Many descendants of the first group of Catholic and Jewish immigrants who had come in before the Civil War now were prosperous second- and third-generation Americans, demanding the right of access to high-status institutions. Other pressures during the 1890's came from increasing immigration from Europe and rapid industrialization and urbanization. In addition, the economic depression of 1893, leading to increased competition for scarce jobs, further stimulated the growth of the APA among the fearful Protestant working class, which constituted a large part of the APA's membership at its height. The APA for the most part worked in and through the Republican Party (although in some areas it also received support from Populist leaders), much as some previous anti-Catholic, nativist movements had worked in and through the Whig Party.

The APA, like the Know-Nothings, flourished for only three or four years. It declined in large part because the Republican leadership, many of whom had encouraged it while the Democrats were in power, turned against it after their overwhelming victories in the depression influenced the 1894 Congressional elections. This success, for which the APA tried to claim credit, suggested to Republican Party leaders like Mark Hanna that they had an opportunity to win over the urban Catholic and immigrant vote if they disassociated themselves from bigoted groups like the APA.

This repudiation of the APA by leading Republicans, some of whom, like McKinley, had earlier encouraged it, illustrates an oft-recurring pattern in the political life of the United States: the moderate conservatives (Whigs or Republicans) when at a low political ebb occasionally encouraged racism or political extremism—overtly or covertly—as a way of winning over some of the less privileged among their Democratic opponents. Such alliances were usually short-lived, since the moderates typically turned on the extremists following either electoral success or the growing revulsion against the increasingly overt bigotry of the extremists.

While anti-Catholicism was the main source of religious bigotry in the nineteenth century, anti-Semitism, which was to become so important in the twentieth century, was also beginning to send up visible shoots. Growing out of the soil of rural America, particularly in the West, anti-Semitism first appeared in political literature in the United States in the 1870's as part of the agrarian response to the depression of 1873. Agrarian protest organizations blamed the decline of farm prices and the other economic difficulties of farmers on the banks, which manipulated the value of money, held farm mortgages, and charged high interest in the New York and international exchanges. In the late nineteenth century the international bankers who controlled these banks were often personified as Jews, and financiers like the Rothschilds were treated as symbols of evil. The literature of the agrarian-based Populist Party of the 1890's sometimes talked darkly of international financial conspiracies designed to destroy

America; some of the Populist leaders were overt anti-Semites as well as active APA members.

Like the Know-Nothings, the APA had considerable strength in urban areas among workers, including trade unionists, particularly in Western states. Eugene Victor Debs, then a railroad union leader, found it necessary to wage a campaign against the divisive influence of the APA within union ranks. Populism, though in some communities linked to the APA, in general, constituted an alternative form of protest for rural, evangelical Protestants in the Midwest and South against the urban, cosmopolitan Eastern elites. Despite occasional expressions of anti-Catholicism and anti-Semitism, the Populists on the whole defined the source of conspiracy which threatened their livelihood and social system in more specifically economic class terms, i.e., the activities of bankers and businessmen. In a sense, both the APA and the Populists expressed the tendency of provincial Americans to regard the culturally and economically dominant Eastern centers as dens of iniquity and economic exploitation. The process of pitting provincial Protestant Americans against secularized wealthy urban elites has been a continuous one in the political life of this country. As part of this process, after the turn of the century, some former Populists shifted their target from urban elites generally to the city-dwelling Catholics and Jews specifically.

The most prominent exponent of this new theme of bigotry was Tom Watson, who had been the major Populist Party leader in the South. Watson had opposed the merger of the Populists with the Democrats in 1896. In various newspapers he continued the Populist diatribes against bankers, capitalists, and railroad magnates, but also increasingly expounded a violent form of racial and religious bigotry directed at Catholics, Jews, and Negroes. Watson's paper, *The Jeffersonian*, published in a small town in Georgia and circulated widely throughout the country, broadcast his contention that Jews and Catholics were united in a conspiracy to take over America. Watson became best known before the United States entered World War I for his leadership in the effort to convict and later lynch an Atlanta Jew, Leo Franks, for the murder of a young girl. Watson seized on this case, and particularly on the efforts of Jews and liberals to defend Franks, as proof of the conspiracy of wealthy Jews to use and mistreat poor Christians.

The 1920's: The Klan, Ford, Repressive Legislation

Following World War I, and during the prosperous 1920's, the United States experienced its most drastic period of repression, typified by the rise of the anti-Catholic, anti-Negro, anti-Semitic, and anti-intellectual Ku Klux Klan. The Klan was founded in 1915 by the members of an organization originally set up by Watson to help convict Leo Franks. With an estimated membership in the 1920's of 3 to 6 million, the Klan drew its members not only from the South but from many Northern states, and elected governors, mayors, and legislators all over the country. It received considerable support in the burgeoning cities both in and out of the South—cities growing by virtue of the large number of recent small-town migrants. These migrants sought to preserve the rural values of their upbringing and saw in the Klan a means to assure "law and order" in their new urban environment.

The Klan charged that Catholics and Jews had allied to dominate the cultural and economic life of the country and that, in conjunction with Communists, they were seeking to seize the government by force.[3] The Klan also revived the

---

3 At this period Negroes were not felt to be as much of a threat as Catholics or Jews; although the Klan was strongly against Negro equality, its attacks of the early 1920's did not fall on Negroes as heavily as on Catholics or Jews.

charges that Catholics had been involved in the killings of Presidents Lincoln, Garfield, and McKinley. It even argued that President Harding was murdered in 1923 by a secret undetectable Catholic weapon—presumably proved by the fact that his death certificate read "cause unknown" and no autopsy was performed. (It was generally agreed that Harding died of a coronary embolism.) Anti-Semitism was also a leading Klan *leitmotif*. One Klan leader held that Jewish international bankers were responsible for starting World War I; others charged that the Jews had organized the Bolshevik Revolution and were behind Communism everywhere. Some Klan leaders combined the Catholic and Jewish conspiratorial themes, suggesting that Jews and Catholics were united in a plan to control the nation's press, economy, and political life. They pointed to New York as an example of a depraved city controlled by Jews and Catholics.

Given the concern with changing values, new, "freer" ideas, and the loss of religious values, it is not surprising that Klan leaders also attacked intellectuals, whom they identified with the growth of "liberalism." They were described by a Klan leader as "one of the chief menaces of the country, instead of the sane intellectual leaders they should be. They give an almost joyous welcome to alien criticism of everything American."

Although the Klan attacked immigrants and Negroes, who were economically deprived, it did not see itself as a conservative defender of white Protestant privileges. Rather, according to Emerson Loucks, the most successful Klan spokesmen consistently appealed to prospective followers by treating "the native white Protestant not as belonging to the predominant and controlling group . . . but as the oppressed poor, oppressed sufferer, plundered by foreigners, tricked by 'Jesuits' and robbed of his birthright by scheming descendants of Abraham." Ironically, they, too, appealed to "the sympathy generally shown by the mass of Americans to the underdog, the fellow they feel hasn't had a fair chance." Thus, the Klan, like its predecessors from the anti-Masons on, linked itself to the anti-elitist and equalitarian tradition of the country while spreading bigotry.

The 1920's also saw the emergence of Henry Ford as a respected spokesman for right-wing extremism and religious prejudice. Through his violently anti-Semitic newspaper, the *Dearborn Independent,* Ford reached more than 700,000 readers. For years, the *Dearborn Independent* hammered away at the theme of an international Jewish conspiracy. A series of eighty articles in the paper were reprinted in book form as *The International Jew: The World's Foremost Problem.* More than 500,000 copies of this extremely anti-Semitic book were distributed throughout the United States. The articles in it bore such titles as "Jewish Gamblers Corrupt American Baseball," "How the Jewish Song Trust Makes You Sing," "Jew Wires Direct Tammany's Gentile Puppets," "The Scope of Jewish Dictatorship in America," "The Jewish Associates of Benedict Arnold." In short, Ford blamed the Jews for everything from Communism to jazz, immorality, and short skirts.

Ford would not be of much interest to the story of political prejudice had he not been boomed as a possible Presidential candidate in 1923. Then at the height of his well-publicized campaign of anti-Semitism, he was widely supported across the country. In fact, one of the early opinion polls reported that 35 per cent of its respondents preferred Ford for President.

Henry Ford's activities dramatized the entry into the American political arena of full-scale anti-Semitism. The Jews were eminently vulnerable to the new turn in conspiracy theory: they were visible in both radical and capitalist circles, although their numbers were wildly exaggerated. They were also castigated in the contemporary conspiracy theories that had been spawned for political purposes in Germany and in tsarist Russia.

It is interesting to note the continuity in the conspiracy literature of the right. The Ku Klux Klan reprinted and circulated many books and stories about Catholic activities which had originated with the Know-Nothings or their predecessors. Ford and the Klan repeated reports about the efforts of Jewish international bankers to control and undermine the American financial system, which first emerged among the agrarian and Populist movements of the 1870's and 1890's. Most interesting of all were the renewed references to the conspiracy of the Illuminati. The staid *Christian Science Monitor* published an editorial in 1920, "A Jewish Peril?" which seriously discussed for a column and a half whether the Elders of Zion or the Illuminati were behind various revolutionary events and political turmoil from Russia to America. The *Dearborn Independent* reminded its readers that on two occasions in early American history men had become aware that the country was threatened by hidden conspiratorial forces, i.e., in 1798, when the Illuminati had first been attacked, and in the late 1820's during the campaign against the Masons. Ford's paper, however, argued that these earlier campaigns had failed because they had not realized that the true conspirators were the Jews, the Illuminati being only a front for the Elders of Zion.

The 1920's not only had its extremist movements, such as the Klan, and its extremist political figures, such as Henry Ford; it also wrote its racial, ethnic, and religious bigotry and its moral absolutism into law. Thus, the period between the end of World War I and the mid-1920's saw the enactment of restrictive immigration legislation that not only limited the total number of immigrants very drastically but also set national quotas which clearly discriminated against people of non-Northern European, non-Protestant background; the Prohibition Amendment, outlawing alcoholic beverages; state laws barring people from wearing religious garb in schools that received tax exemptions; and laws prohibiting the teaching of evolution, particularly in the South.

All this legislation represented a significant victory for the forces of fundamentalism, nativism, xenophobia, and moralism. Efforts to bring about such nativist and moralist restrictions have a long history going back almost to the beginning of the republic, but until the 1920's they achieved no widespread legislative success. Why should these crusades have won out in the 1920's? Why did the United States succumb at that time to a wave of repressive nationalist, moralistic, puritanical hysteria? There is no way, of course, to answer these questions with absolute certainty, but the analyses of this period by historians and social scientists suggest that these rightist actions represented the fear of many groups that persistent social change was finally destroying the kind of America they believed in, the Protestant America in which they had been reared.

Perhaps the most palpable sign of such social change was the growth of the cities. The rural-urban rivalry cited earlier was made much more pointed by the rapidly increasing urbanization of the country. The 1920 census reported that for the first time the rural population had become a minority in the United States. The big cities were the centers of communications and of visible cultural influence. They were also the centers of settlement of the tremendous waves of immigrants who had come from the non-Protestant areas of Europe. Most of the immigration from the 1890's to World War I was Catholic, Orthodox Christian, or Jewish. Relatively little, proportionate to the total group, came from Northern European Protestant countries. By World War I and after, this influx was reflected in the visibly growing political power of

Catholics through the urban Democratic machines, and in the power of the rising Jewish middle class. The cities that dominated the economic and political life of the country seemed to be controlled by the large numbers of non-Protestant immigrants. The rapidly growing cities, of course, contained large numbers of Protestants, many of them workers who had migrated from rural areas. This group provided the Klan with a considerable low-status urban base, which resented and resisted the political power of the urban Democratic machines and the cultural liberalism of the urban cosmopolitan elites. And outside the urban areas, the Klan drew strength from evangelical Protestants in small towns and rural areas who began to feel that they were isolated provincials, far from the mainstream, while the cities were controlled by elites with different values, attitudes, and customs. As one Ku Klux Klan leader poignantly put it, "We have become strangers in the land of our fathers."

The earlier pre–twentieth century expressions of mass bigotry and belief in conspiracy theories had each arisen during periods marked by the sharp decline of the party supported by evangelical Protestants, Federalists, Whigs, and Republicans. The year 1920 marked a drastic shift in party fortunes, but this time it was the Republican Party that gained. The conservative restorative politics of Warren Harding were endorsed by more than 60 per cent of the electorate, the largest percentage ever received by a Republican, while the incumbent Democrats garnered little more than a third of the vote. Although the Klan in many Northern states largely worked with or within the Republican Party, partisan weakness was clearly not a source of Klan strength. Rather it would appear that the rise of the Klan, the appeal of Henry Ford, and the massive increase in Republican support, each reflected in different ways the desire of many Americans to restore values of a rural moralistic Protestant society to an America changed by war, urbanization, and heavy waves of non-Nordic immigration.

The Republican Party adapted to this shift in mood of its supporters. Campaigning for the Presidency in 1920, Warren Harding spoke of the dangers to America inherent in "racial differences," and recommended that the United States should only admit immigrants whose background indicated that they could develop "a full consecration to American practices and ideas." His Vice-President and successor as President, Calvin Coolidge, wrote shortly before the new administration took office in 1921 that "biological laws show that Nordics deteriorate when mixed with other races." James J. Davis, Harding's and Coolidge's Secretary of Labor, went even further to argue for immigration restrictions on the ground that the older Nordic "immigrants to America were the beaver type who built up America, whereas the newer immigrants were rat-men trying to tear it down; and obviously rat-men could never become beavers." The third of the trio of Republican Presidents of the 1920's, Herbert Hoover, also joined in the chorus at the beginning of the decade, when, speaking as Secretary of Commerce, he declared that "immigrants now lived in the United States on sufferance . . . and would be tolerated only if they behaved."

In reaction to a growing sense of displacement, the Protestant nonmetropolitan Republicans of the North joined with the Protestant Democrats in the South against the big city Democrats in the 1920's. This first Dixiecrat-Republican coalition led to the passage of Prohibition, restrictions on immigration, and other repressive legislation already mentioned. Although their successes could be taken as indices of the strength of these provincial and evangelical Protestant groups, it is probably more accurate to regard them as reflecting a backlash occurring at the very time when these interest groups were losing out. During the nineteenth century most Americans could have been described as white, Protestant rural people or small-town residents. Yet, during the time that they constituted an overwhelming majority, their more extreme beliefs—nativist, fundamentalist, Prohibition-ist—were not massively incorporated into legislation. It was only as the group was declining, as it began to see other groups and other values taking over, that the necessary im-petus—in this case, fear—was provided to enact these values into law.

The rights of dissenters got short shrift during this period. On federal, state, and local levels, official actions limited the rights of political opposition through explicit legislation, legislative investigations, and administrative fiat. In the hunt for radicals, the Department of Justice was guilty of illegal search and seizure, of intimidating interrogation, of levying excessive bail, and of denial of counsel. Official action was matched by repressive private action, which included tarring and feathering, and in some instances, lynching political offenders. These offenders were typically regarded as being of the "wrong" color, the "wrong" religion, the "wrong" ethnic stock.

The hysteria of the 1920's gradually died away. It died partly because, as in the case of the Klan, the causes which it espoused were relatively successful. It declined also because its excesses, its use of violence, led the more respectable ele-ments who had either supported or tolerated it in its early period to drop away and help turn the hose of community social pressure on it. The Klan lost much of its middle-class support by 1924, and remained as a declining organization of less educated workers and farmers. It failed finally because this movement—like the APA and the Know-Nothings be-fore it—was composed of extremists who tended to turn on each other in a bitter, aggressive, and paranoid way and thus to split up. The last gasp of the bigotry of the 1920's was the highly prejudicial anti-Catholic campaign against the Presidential candidacy of Al Smith in 1928.

As in the case of previous mass expressions of bigotry, the hysteria proved hard to maintain beyond a few years, but the legislation enacted during the 1920's had long-lasting effects. Prohibition continued until 1933, with disastrous consequences for attitudes toward law and order. Biased immigration quotas lasted until just a few years ago. Although much of the politically restrictive legislation has been voided by the Supreme Court, some of it still remains on the books.

Neo-Fascist Movements of the 1930's

The decade of the 1930's—with its massive economic depression, unemployment, and political pressures linked to revolutionary events in Europe—witnessed its share of extremist movements. Both left-wing and right-wing groups gained adherents in this difficult period. The list of rightist neo-Fascist movements is almost endless: the Silver Shirts of William Pelley, the Midwestern Black Legion, the Christian Defenders of Gerald Winrod, the Union for Social Justice of Father Coughlin, the Committee of One Million of Gerald L. K. Smith, and so on. No one knows how many active members these groups had or how many others agreed with them.

Studies of the support of these groups indicate that they appealed heavily to the more religious, less educated, and more provincial elements among both Protestants and Catholics. Their conspiratorial charges were directed mainly against Jews and Communists but occasionally also against Catholics. Gerald Winrod, a principal Protestant fundamentalist figure, was pro-Nazi and virulently anti-Catholic and anti-Semitic, and was given to ominous warnings about the plots of the Elders of Zion.

The most important of these right-wing extremists was the

Catholic priest, Charles Coughlin. The Coughlinite movement demonstrated that many Catholics could hate just as
well as Protestants could. Openly anti-Semitic and increasingly pro-Fascist, Father Coughlin had an audience of millions for his weekly radio program. Reliable opinion polling,
which began in the mid-1930's, showed that Coughlin's views
were endorsed by more than 25 per cent of the adult population. His ideology sounded leftist to many since he strongly
opposed private ownership of the banks and placed the responsibility for the Great Depression on the desire for profit
of international bankers, most of whom were identified as
Jews.

It is interesting that both Winrod and Coughlin believed
that the Illuminati, the same society which supposedly had
organized the French Revolution, had fostered the emergence
of many subsequent revolutionary movements, including the
Russian Revolution, and now influenced the New Deal.
Winrod, however, identified the Illuminati as the source of a
Jesuit-Jewish alliance to dominate the world. Coughlin naturally did not speak of Catholic involvement, but he did link
the Illuminati, and occasionally the Masons, with the efforts
of the Elders of Zion and other Jewish groups to advance
Communism.

The high point of Coughlin's support was attained early in
1936. His organization, the National Union for Social Justice,
probably had close to a million members and reached out
through organized groups to most of the country: Coughlin
also had a much larger population listening sympathetically
to his weekly broadcasts. Most Congressional candidates endorsed by Coughlin in the 1936 primaries won their nomina-
tion fights. He disrupted the base of his support, however, by
trying to turn his movement into a third party, the Union
Party, behind the Presidential candidacy of William Lemke.
By so doing, Coughlin ran into the perennial difficulty of

such efforts: their inability to prevent sympathetic voters from backing the "lesser evil" between the two major party choices. In this case, many underprivileged Coughlinites who were benefiting from the extensive programs of the New Deal, chose to vote for Franklin Roosevelt. Lemke, who had the backing of 8 per cent of the electorate in July according to the Gallup Poll, wound up with less than 2 per cent of the vote. Coughlin, thereupon, dissolved his National Union organization and temporarily withdrew from politics. Although he returned soon after, forming new but much smaller organizations of supporters and voicing much more explicit and virulent racist appeals, he never recovered from the failure of the Union Party campaign.

In the latter years of the 1930's, the Coughlinites and the myriad of other bigoted movements strongly opposed American intervention in World War II, since they tended to support the Nazis. Indeed, various opinion surveys indicate that close to half the population had strong anti-Semitic attitudes at a time when the Nazis were riding high in Europe. But the impact of Pearl Harbor and in some cases direct government action killed these movements during World War II.

The Cold War Era and Joseph McCarthy

Following the war, racial tensions and concern with Communism supplanted anti-Catholicism and anti-Semitism as the most salient sources of conspiratorial belief. The major racist efforts in this postwar period date from the Supreme Court's desegregation decision in 1954. That decision prompted the formation of White Citizens' Councils and other groups aimed at throttling the struggle for Negro equality. The most prominent right-wing movement of the early 1950's, however, was *not* racist. It was the anti-Communist movement spearheaded by Senator Joseph McCarthy which emerged in 1950. Mc-

Carthy tended to concentrate his attention on the conspiratorial sources of the failures of American foreign policy; these failures, he claimed, represented the work of undetected Communist agents who had infiltrated both the government and the key opinion-forming and policy-controlling institutions of the society. McCarthy alleged that these agents were particularly strong among the social elite, the graduates of Groton and Harvard, those who ran the newspapers, professors in the universities, the heads of the foundations, the personnel of the State Department, and so on. He thus appealed to the status strains of many socially and economically inferior segments of the society and transposed into a new key the conspiracy theme that has characterized so much of American extremist politics. Analysis of opinion poll data bearing on support for McCarthy's activities indicated that they came disproportionately from the less privileged strata, especially those among his Catholic coreligionists, and from ethnic groups (German and Irish) and sections of the country (the Midwest particularly) that had been opposed to American entry into World War II.

Again, typifying the conservative party's repeated reaction to extremist groups, many moderate Republican leaders generally encouraged McCarthy before 1953, seeing in his activities an opportunity to win the support of many underprivileged Democrats, particularly Catholics, who reacted strongly against the rise of Communism abroad and the seeming decline of American world power. Richard Rovere has suggested that this behavior was a consequence of Republican reaction to Truman's unanticipated victory over Dewey in the 1948 elections. Republican Congressional triumphs in 1946, plus optimistic reports from the opinion polls, had led party leaders to anticipate that after sixteen years in opposition, they were about to take office. Defeat, following on this sharp increase in their level of expectation, undermined their commitment to the conventional rules of the political game, and led them, like the Federalists and Whigs earlier, to tolerate or encourage the use of extremist tactics. Victory in the 1952 elections ended their need to rely on such measures. McCarthy's insistence on continuing his attack against the governmental elite, now in the hands of Republicans, ultimately resulted in his censure in 1954 by the Senate. Thereafter, he almost totally disappeared from sight; the mass media, which had given extensive publicity to his attacks, simply stopped covering him. His mass support, which also declined, may have been responding to these changes at the elite level, as well as to the end of the Korean War, which occurred about the same time.

The John Birch Society in the 1960's

After the McCarthy movement collapsed, a host of smaller right-wing groups emerged. Some of them have focused on the Jews and Communists and have charged that the civil rights movements and efforts to improve the situations of Negroes are part of a Jewish-Communist conspiracy. However, the most publicized movement of the 1960's, the John Birch Society, has not been anti-Semitic, but it strongly opposes the civil rights movement. It has subscribed to conspiracy theory, identifying many of the economic and social trends that it opposes as a consequence of the efforts of a "hidden conspiracy of Insiders," i.e., our old friends, the Illuminati. The Birch Society attributes both the rise of the welfare state and the growth of the civil rights movement to an alleged Illuminati-controlled Communist conspiracy.

In his pamphlet, *The Truth in Time,* Robert Welch, the head of the Society, credits the Illuminati with being responsible for both World Wars, the Russian Revolution, the breakup of the colonial empires, the formation of the United Nations, centralized banking, the personal income tax, the direct election of Senators in the United States, and "everything in the way of 'security' legislation, from the first Workmen's Compensation Acts under Bismarck to the latest Medicare monstrosity under Lyndon Johnson." Like Henry Ford, Welch sees continuity both in the conspiracy and in the opposition to it. Thus he identifies with the anti-Masonic movement of the early nineteenth century, stating that just as the Illuminati killed William Morgan, an opponent of Freemasonry whose kidnapping and disappearance in 1826 led to the formation of the anti-Masonic movement, they had also eliminated Senator Joseph McCarthy when he became aware of their activities.

In an unsigned introduction to a 1967 Birch Society edition of John Robison's book, *Proofs of a Conspiracy,* first published in 1798, the Society makes clear who it thinks the Illuminati were and are:

> This was a conspiracy conceived, organized and activated by professionals and intellectuals, many of them brilliant, but cunning and clever, who decided to put their minds in the service of total evil. . . . One tends to think of professors, philosophers and writers as sitting in their ivory towers, perfectly harmless to the world. Robison and history proved otherwise. . . . From Woodrow Wilson—himself a professor—to Lyndon Johnson, we have had nothing but Presidents surrounded by professors and scholars. . . . All of which brings to mind Weishaupt's plan to surround the ruling authorities with members of his Order.

And in discussing the current activities of the Illuminati, the Birch Society Introduction states that they no longer espouse Freemasonry. "Their main habitat these days seems to be the great subsidized universities, tax-free foundations, mass media communication systems, and a myriad of private organizations, such as the Council on Foreign Relations."

The Society on the whole, eschews appeals to religious and racial bigotry, placing the brunt of its attack on the Illuminati and their Communist agents. It has expelled various members and some prominent leaders for anti-Semitic activities and statements. Although strongly against any efforts to foster civil rights or improve the socio-economic conditions of the black population through governmental action, it seeks to find conservative Negroes whose activities it can identify with and support. The tenor of its attacks on the civil rights movement, however, frequently leads Birchers to write and speak about Negroes in terms that can only be described as racist. It also strongly supports the rights of white minorities to rule in South Africa and Rhodesia on the grounds that they constitute the only real alternative to Communism or anarchy.

Given its strong ideological attack on all forms of the welfare state and trade unionism, the Society has little or no appeal for the underprivileged. Analyses of its members and sympathizers indicate that it derives its support from a relatively affluent, well-educated stratum. Seemingly, according to studies of the Society's membership by Fred Grupp, Murray Havens, and Burton Levy, they come from the less prestigious segment of the affluent, those who did not finish college or went to inferior ones. Their top leaders tend to be heads of family-owned corporations located in relatively small provincial cities. Like the APA and the Klan, Birch Society chapters are more likely to be found in rapidly expanding communities, particularly in the South and West.

The combination of deep conspiratorial and ultraconservative dogma has meant that the organization has remained relatively small (possibly 60,000 members at its height in 1965) and unpopular. Recognizing the difficulty of gaining wide support for the Society's full program, Robert Welch, its founder and head, has defined its role as that of a vanguard organization modeling its tactics on that of the Communists, i.e., using "front organizations" in which Birch members can play controlling roles.

The American Independent Party—1968

The largest and most important contemporary movement linked to racial concerns has been the American Independent Party, headed by Governor George Wallace, who ran for President in 1968. Almost every extreme right-wing group, almost every virulent racist in the country backed Wallace. He produced a coalition of the right such as probably never existed before, at least in the twentieth century. Birch Society members, in particular, played a leading role in the Wallace party and campaign organization in many states. In both his 1964 campaign in the Democratic Presidential primaries and in his recent third party effort, Wallace made strong pro-Birch Society statements. His campaign speeches were clear, simple, and insistent. Although he rarely mentioned Negroes as such, he campaigned strongly against government legislation that in any way involves enforcing integration or civil rights with respect to open housing, schools, unions, etc. He also spoke frequently about the need for force to deal with the breakdown in law and order, crime in the streets, and riots. Other frequent themes in his speeches dealt with fear of central government power generally and a concern for American weakness abroad, particularly as reflected in the inability to win the Vietnamese war.

Unlike the Birch Society, however, which is explicitly elitist, Wallace directed an appeal to the common man of America who, he has argued, is brighter and more moral than the elite. His heroes are the taxi driver, the steel worker, the auto mechanic and the little man generally. He sees the "pseudo-intellectuals"—college professors, the heads of the "tax-free" foundations, editors of leading newspapers and magazines, members of the Council on Foreign Relations, and high-ranking bureaucrats in Washington—as the source of evil and propagators of false doctrine. (This characterization of the pseudo-intellectuals closely resembles descriptions of the Illuminati in Birch Society literature.) Coming out of a Southern Populist tradition, Wallace suggests the existence of an elitist conspiracy based on the Eastern Establishment. Thus, during the campaign he argued that the public opinion polls were being deliberately manipulated against him by the "Eastern money interests." Taking a leaf out of Senator Joseph McCarthy's book, he has identified Communism with the well-to-do rather than with the down-and-out, stating: "I don't believe all this talk about poor folks turning Communist. It's the damn rich who turn Communist. You ever seen a poor Communist?"

Strongly antagonistic to the federal judiciary for its rulings on integration and on the rights of Communists and of defendants in criminal cases, Wallace proposed the plan first suggested by the Populists of the 1890's—the direct election of federal judges. This solution reiterates his repeated emphasis on the moral and intellectual superiority of the common man.

Wallace's movement is not to be taken lightly. In the 1968 election, Wallace received the support of 13 per cent of the electorate. It was the first time in half a century that a third party had been on the ballot in every state, indicating the degree of organization and competency of this movement. The strength of Wallace's appeal was even greater than the vote he received indicates. Both the Gallup and Harris Polls reported at the end of September that 21 per cent of the electorate preferred him to Humphrey or Nixon. As Election Day approached, the Wallace support in the polls declined steadily as many of his supporters, recognizing that he could not win, began to feel the pressure to vote for the "lesser evil."

Yet Wallace was able to retain more of his backing against such pressure than any other third party candidate in almost half a century. And it should be noted that when the Gallup Poll inquired on a number of occasions in 1968 not how people intended to vote, but whether they approved or disapproved generally of George Wallace, more than 40 per cent indicated approval. But even if the election showing represents his maximum support—Wallace's more than 9 million votes represent a substantial following.

Wallace finds his support among the same social strata as those that backed the earlier movements. They are disproportionately rural or small-town dwellers and Protestants (although he has considerable strength among Catholics). They are likely to be less educated and poorer than the population at large. Outside of white Southern racist support, the largest segment of his backing in the 1968 election came from manual workers, many of them trade unionists. A special national poll of union members conducted by the Gallup organization for *The New York Times* early in October reported that 25 per cent supported Wallace. A referendum conducted within the United Automobile Workers among elected local and regional *officers* found more than 10 per cent choosing the American Independent Party nominee. A number of trade union locals in the North actually endorsed his candidacy. Journalists reported deep concern on the part of union leaders about their memberships' enthusiasm for Wallace. The unions reacted to this situation by devoting more energy and money to influencing their members' votes than in any previous election. Evidence from polls indicates that these efforts succeeded in turning many of Wallace's supporters back to their traditional party allegiance, although, proportionally, more manual workers than middle-class people voted for Wallace.

Many of these workers who are steadily employed are purchasing their own homes in neighborhoods that are relatively close to expanding black areas, are bothered by higher taxes, and are opposed to the welfare program as a system that taxes the hard-working to help the lazy and the unfit. To a considerable extent they identify these with the Negroes. Since white union members are much more likely than the more affluent middle class to live inside the central cities, they are also more directly and personally concerned with the problem of increased urban crime and with efforts at integrating urban school systems through modifying the concept of the neighborhood school. Many workers see the pressures for school desegregation as coming from the well-educated middle class, which lives in the suburbs or sends its children to private schools. The issue for them has become the well-to-do forcing the white working class to send its children to school with black children.

The disproportionate support given to George Wallace by workers, a phenomenon akin to the backing received by the Know-Nothings, the APA, the Ku Klux Klan, the Coughlinite Christian Front, and Senator Joseph McCarthy, contradicts the assumption of many who identify the working class and trade unionism with support for progressive social objectives. This phenomenon of working-class endorsement of bigotry *and* of trade unionism and the welfare state coincides with the results of various sociological surveys that have found that the less educated (and, therefore, also poorer) people are, the more likely they are to be prejudiced against minority groups and to be intolerant of deviance generally. Conversely, however, the less well-to-do a group, the more disposed it is to favor liberal-left policies with regard to such issues as trade unions, social security, economic planning, and the like. Workers and the less affluent generally vote for liberal-left parties because they see these parties as defenders of their economic and class interests against the conservatives, who are identified in their minds with the well-to-do and big business. A candidate who seeks to appeal to their racial sentiments, but is also visibly opposed to their economic interests, such as Barry Goldwater in 1964, cannot gain their votes.

George Wallace, however, shied away from such positions and sought to identify the pressures for Negro equality and integration with the Eastern Establishment and the intellectual elite. Not being a Republican also probably helped his image with many workers. They can more easily vote for a candidate and party that appeals to the common man than for a candidate and party identified with the wealthy. And Wallace did make a direct appeal for such support on economic lines by calling for a sharp increase in Social Security payments and for doubling the personal exemption on the income tax, a change which would particularly benefit the less affluent. His party platform also proposed liberalizing payments under the Medicare program. (It may be significant to note that the Harris Poll reported that many more Wallace supporters in the North chose the term "radical" to describe his political outlook than identified him as "conservative.") The opinion analyst, Samuel Lubell, reported in late October that "Pro-Wallace supporters in the northern cities . . . voice strong working-class views which prevent them from voting Republican. . . . Most of these Wallace followers maintain, 'Wallace is for the workingman. He couldn't be for anyone else.' Some even talk of the Wallace movement as 'the start of a new labor party.' "

One relatively low-status occupation group reported as heavily involved in the ranks of Wallace supporters is policemen. In this respect also, the American Independent Party resembles its predecessors on the extreme right. Data bearing on the membership of the American Protective Association in the 1890's, of the Ku Klux Klan of the 1920's and 1950's, of the Black Legion and the Coughlinite Christian Front of the 1930's, and of the Birch Society in the 1960's, have indicated the disproportionate presence of policemen in their ranks.

A number of elements in the social background and work experience of the police predisposes them to racial bigotry. As Gunnar Myrdal noted almost three decades ago, they tend to be recruited from the lower-status and less educated segments of the population. A recent study of the New York police describes the typical recruit as being of "working-class background, high school education or less, average intelligence, cautious personality." Prejudice against Negroes is greater among persons with such backgrounds. Police work tends to reinforce and intensify such feelings, since it brings policemen into contact with the worst elements in the Negro community.

The policeman's role is also particularly subject to creating feelings of resentment against society flowing from status discrepancies. On the one hand, he is given considerable authority by society to enforce its laws and is expected to risk his life if necessary; on the other, he receives little prestige and a relatively low salary. A number of studies report the police complaint that they are not respected by the public. Overt hostility and even contempt for the police often are voiced by spokesmen for liberal and left groups and intellectuals. Insofar as the police find any segment of the body politic that shows appreciation for their contribution to society and the risks they take, it is the conservatives, and particularly the far right. Thus, the slogan "Support your local police" was enunciated by the Ku Klux Klan in the early 1920's, revived by the Birch Society in the 1960's, and placed on the auto license plates of the state of Alabama by George Wallace when he was governor. The Birch Society has established awards for heroic policemen and has set up a fund for the support of the families of police killed in the line of duty. George Wallace went out of his way in campaign speeches to praise the police and to denounce their liberal intellectual critics.

Within the strata that disproportionately backed George Wallace, young people have been prevalent. Gallup and Harris surveys reported in October that 25 per cent, one out of every four between twenty-one and twenty-nine years old, were for Wallace, as contrasted with 20 per cent among the older groups. This phenomenon of disproportionate youth support for an extremist racist candidate has largely been ignored by those who have identified young America with left-wing campus demonstrators and student volunteers for Kennedy and McCarthy. In a real sense, the New Right of George Wallace, like the New Left, is a direct outgrowth of a process of political polarization that emerged around the desegregation efforts since the late 1950's. Many of the liberal white university students who joined the civil rights movement began to despair of American democracy when they witnessed authority in the South violating the law in order to preserve segregation. The tactics of civil disobedience and sit-ins first emerged among the student left as a response to the civil disobedience initiated by such white segregationist leaders as Ross Barnett of Mississippi, Lester Maddox of Georgia, and George Wallace of Alabama. At the same time, however, many white youth in the South and in urban working-class areas of the North grew up during a period in which the issue of integration within their schools and communities has been salient. They were reared in an atmosphere in which the voicing of anti-Negro sentiments in their homes and neighborhoods was common, in which members of the older generation discussed their fears concerning the adverse consequences of school or residential integration. Hence, while the upper middle-class scions of liberal parents were being radicalized to the left, Southern and Northern working-class youth were being radicalized to the right. The consequences of such polarization can be seen in the behavior of the two groups in the 1968 election campaign.

The indications that the Wallace movement draws heavily from among youth are congruent with the evidence from various studies of youth and student politics that young people are disposed to support the more extreme or idealistic version of the politics dominant within their social group. In Europe, radical movements of both the left and the right have been much more likely to secure the backing of the young than have the democratic parties of the center. Being less committed to existing institutions and parties than older people, being less inured to the need to compromise to achieve objectives, youth are attracted to movements and leaders who promise to resolve basic problems quickly in an absolute fashion. Unfortunately, as yet few data exist bearing on the extent to which the earlier American rightist movements also drew support from youth.

The Implications of the Wallace Movement

The conclusion that concern over race and the related issue of "law and order" were the dominant preoccupations among Wallace voters was borne out by the national opinion surveys. The pollster Louis Harris reported that "The common bond that sews together this unusual assortment of political allies in this election is dominantly race. A heavy 73 per cent of all Wallace supporters want progress for Negroes to be halted. Almost as many, 67 per cent, say that they 'feel uneasy personally due to the prospect of race riots in their own community.' "

Feeling about racial issues is not, of course, the only factor that has fostered the emergence of a New Right. The Wallace movement has disproportionate support among farmers and residents of small towns, who are rarely in contact with

Negroes. Many in these groups appear to be responding to a concern over the changes in American religious and cultural beliefs. They are often religious or secular fundamentalists. They oppose changes in that old-time religion or in the traditional American individualist way of life. The religious fundamentalists, concentrated in rural areas and small towns, or among migrants from such places to big cities, feel deprived by the fact that American society has become cosmopolitan and metropolitan. Fundamentalist values are treated as provincial and anachronistic by those who control the mass media and the cultural life of the nation. These cultural trends, of course, have intensified with the passage of time and to a considerable extent now dominate the major theological camps within both Protestantism and Catholicism. This now definitely minority group of traditionalist Christians has become a principal source of support for a politics of alienation and nostalgia. And to the resentments of the religious fundamentalists are joined those of many not particularly religious people who are deeply disturbed by changes in secular values.

It should be noted, however, that except among the minority of committed extremists, the Wallace movement as such failed to make headway with the bulk of affluent and better educated upper- and middle-class conservatives. A national opinion survey by *The New York Times* in mid-October of the presidents of *all* the companies whose shares are listed in the New York Stock Exchange, conducted by the anonymous questionnaire technique, reported that less than half of 1 per cent (three men) were for Wallace, while 85 per cent endorsed Nixon, and 13 per cent backed Humphrey. While Wallace had more support in lower levels of the business and professional community, particularly in the South, it is clear from the polls that this stratum was also disproportionately opposed to him. Most of these people, though economic conservatives, are not afraid that the country is being taken over by Negroes or other minority groups and are not alienated from the body politic. Insofar as they are politically motivated, they are active in the Republican Party. In California, they united in 1966 behind Ronald Reagan, who embodies these conservative virtues. On a local and Congressional level they could find many candidates with kindred opinions within the GOP in 1968. Richard Nixon, who supported Goldwater in 1964 and who in turn was strongly supported by him before the Republican Convention in 1968, though not as conservative as some of them would have liked, still was sufficiently close to such views to retain their support.

The Wallace movement clearly is not a conservative tendency. Rather, it is a movement of the alienated adherents of religious and secular fundamentalism. It appeals to those who really feel threatened by the rise of the Negro in the cities, by the changes in the moral order which they can witness nightly on television, by the changing content of Protestantism and Catholicism, by miniskirts, and by the decline of the United States on the world scene. There are millions of such frustrated individuals in America today. George Wallace has found a way of reaching many of them. In a real sense, he is trying to build a Poujadist movement out of those who reject "modernism."

The reactionary movements of the 1960's—the Wallace movement, the Birch Society, the Christian Crusade of Billy James Hargis, and others—resemble the backlash politics that swept the country in the 1920's. Today as then, many continue to be out of step with the dominant cultural trends of the society and to feel bitter about the decline of traditional Christian morality. It remains to be seen how powerful they will be this time. On the one hand, their base of fundamentalists living in small towns and rural areas no longer constitutes the near-majority it did in the 1920's; now it represents only a small minority. But this group has been joined by the scions of the immigrants in the large cities, many of them Catholics, threatened by the inroads made by Negroes. Many of them react today to the growth in urban Negro population much as white Protestant workers reacted to the Catholic immigration in the nineteenth century.

The racial resentments of the provincial fundamentalist Protestants, including many who have moved to large cities, and of the children of immigrants, are playing a major role in the realignment of American politics occurring in the 1960's. Once again their resentments are contributing to the ranks of the more conservative of the two major parties as well as making possible the rise of explicitly racially oriented parties and movements. The fears of these people have been expressed in recent years by many mayoral candidates, such as Louise Day Hicks in Boston, as well as by a number of prominent right-wing Republicans who have appealed to racism indirectly by discussing the dangers of crime in the streets, riots, or open housing legislation. Clearly, though many of them have not openly talked about Negroes and race, they can say, as Mrs. Hicks did, "You know where I stand."

Once again it must be said that a leader of the Republicans, Richard Nixon, has sought to refurbish the strength of his party among traditional Democratic supporters by appealing to those who have shown a readiness to abandon their party allegiance in favor of a racist candidate. As *The New York Times* (October 12, 1968, p. 10E) reported, using "the Wallace slogan, 'Stand up for America,' he lauds Senator Strom Thurmond [the Presidential candidate of an earlier effort to create a third prosegregationist party in 1948] as a man 'who has stood up for his state and will stand up for America and I'm glad to stand with him today.'" Many analysts of the 1968 election have described the campaign tactics of the Republican Vice-Presidential candidate, Spiro Agnew, as an effort to "out-Wallace Wallace." He spoke out repeatedly in strong terms about the need to crack down on threats to law and order, explained the fact that he did not campaign in Negro areas by saying "if you've seen one ghetto area, you've seen them all," described Hubert Humphrey as "soft on Communism," and attacked "phony intellectuals," Wallace's favorite target, "who don't understand what we mean by hard work and patriotism." Since Agnew maintained his Wallace-like posture throughout the campaign, there can be little doubt that he was fulfilling a role assigned to him by party strategists, i.e., to show Wallace supporters that they could get what they wanted from the Republican Party. Thus the major consequence of the Wallace movement may be that it, like the anti-Masonic and the Know-Nothing American parties, will serve as a transmission belt to bring the more bigoted Democrats to the opposition conservative party which adapts its policies to accommodate their concerns.

There is a real danger, however, that George Wallace will try to mobilize his supporters in a new mass movement which, like some of the earlier ones, will engage in extraparliamentary confrontationist tactics, including taking to the streets to intimidate opponents. During the campaign Wallace openly discussed the possibility of a "white revolution" should he fail to win, directed toward forcing the state governments "to physically take over the schools" to end integration. As he described the process, there would first be mass rallies and protest demonstrations throughout the country. The vigor of such protests would press the states to bring about a halt in federal interference in local school policies. Wallace has argued that the common people are ready for drastic action and boasts of the fact that many in his campaign audiences became hysterical when he discussed law and order and school integration. Clearly, Wallace has been toying with the idea of turning his electoral party into a mass movement that will take to the streets to counter the activities of the "anarchists," the demonstrators and rioters in the ghettos and on the campuses. The implications of such an endeavor for the future of democratic politics in the United States are obvious.

As a final evaluative point, it is important to recognize that all of the earlier movements discussed here have been short-lived, even though most of them involved millions of people in their activities. Various analysts have explained their rise as a result of basic endemic tension-creating processes, explanations which imply that some of them should have continued to exist for much longer than they did, since the conditions which supposedly gave rise to them continued while the movements declined or died. Thus, the heyday of the anti-Masons was from 1828–32. The Know-Nothing American Party was able to win elections in many states from 1854–57, but quickly dwindled away thereafter. The American Protective Association became a multimillion member alliance in 1892–94, but disintegrated by 1896. The Ku Klux Klan presumably recruited close to 4 million members between 1921 and 1924 and helped elect many governors and other officials. It was an important force at both major party national conventions in 1924. By 1925 it had lost much of its membership, and by the late 1920's it was a small group. The two largest movements of the 1930's, which had considerable support according to the opinion polls, were Huey Long's Share-Our-Wealth movement and the Coughlinite organizations. Long's movement, which was formed in 1934, totally vanished with his assassination in 1935: his second-in-command, Gerald L. K. Smith, could not find a handful to follow him. Coughlin's high point with respect to membership and popular support occurred in 1936. Thereafter, he led a declining movement, which disappeared into limbo after Pearl Harbor. The phenomenon known as McCarthyism lasted four years, from 1950 to 1954.

Looking over this record suggests the need to determine

not only which conditions prompt different groups of Americans to become disposed to form and join movements that are far outside of the American "consensus" but also why they decline so quickly. Some of them, e.g., the anti-Masons and possibly the Ku Klux Klan, lost out after seemingly achieving their most prominent objectives. Others, like the APA, the Klan, and McCarthyism, lost support after segments of the more established elements that supported them in their early period turned against them. These elements came to oppose the movements either because they had achieved some of *their* objectives—i.e., the political defeat of their opponents—or because extremist tactics make it difficult for respectable individuals to remain identified with them. Some, like the Know-Nothings and the APA, splintered because they included many who differed widely on issues other than the one which brought them into existence. A few, particularly the Klan, declined after it became clear that their leaders were involved in fraudulent activities or had begun to fight among themselves.

Although no one has presented an adequate general explanation for the short-lived character of American protest movements, a few hypotheses can be offered: First, those that have tried the third-party route have been unable to break through the constraints placed on such efforts by the American constitutional structure, which makes of the entire country one constituency for the one important election, that of the Presidency. Like the Know-Nothings in 1856 and the Coughlinites in 1936, they wind up in Presidential elections with much less support than they had previously. One of the major parties usually makes some efforts to appeal to their supporters, and many of them vote for the "lesser evil" on election day. The movements, as distinct from the parties, often attract leaders and activists whose values and personalities make it difficult for them to compromise on new issues facing the group. The intense factional struggles which often arise result in such acrimonious bickering as to discourage many of their members and supporters. Those movements that become more extreme in their tactics often find the more moderate groups withdrawing. The Establishment, in the form of the media, community, church, and political leaders, ultimately unites to place extremist movements that show a capacity to survive outside the pale of socially tolerated activity. But whatever the cause of decline, the fact remains that all such extremist efforts have quickly subsided. And although the social strains that led millions to join or follow these movements presumably continued to exist, efforts to maintain or revive them, once the process of decline has started, have invariably failed.

Political Bigotry in Retrospect and Prospect

This concludes a brief analysis of the appeals that have been made to racial and religious prejudice in efforts to preserve the status or values of groups with a prior claim to the American tradition. The story has been discouraging, but this does not mean that no changes occur. On the positive side one may point to the fact that overt support for bigotry has become much more shamefaced than in the past. No prominent American politician speaks directly about the negative traits of minority groups in the way that leading Whigs and Republicans did in the nineteenth and early twentieth centuries. Lest we forget, it should be noted that the three Republican presidents of the 1920's—Harding, Coolidge, and Hoover—all openly spoke or wrote about the threat to American values posed by Americans of non–Anglo-Saxon backgrounds. Except in the South, no politician dares any longer to attack Negroes as such. Racist appeals, of course, continue, but they now take the form of discussion of the "problems" created by unspecified groups. To the inhabitants of the ghetto such changes may seem trivial, when men can still get elected by appealing to the fears and bigotry of whole sections of the population. Yet the fact that the major party politicians who speak of the problems of law and order also feel obliged to advance a program which is ostensibly designed to improve economic and educational conditions in the ghetto does attest to an improvement in the attitudes of white America. All the opinion polls agree that there has been a decline in expressed antiminority attitudes, whether these are toward Negroes, Catholics, or Jews. It is striking to note, for example, that the religious affiliation of Robert Kennedy and Eugene McCarthy was never mentioned during the 1968 campaign.

Given the existence of institutionalized sources of discrimination, such change in attitudes implies no more than unrealized potential. American institutions are still fundamentally biased in favor of whites, but Americans as a people are closer to expressing a belief in the creed of equality than they have ever been. Whether they believe in it deeply enough to live by it is another question. The struggle for a genuinely equalitarian society is obviously far from having been won. There will be many reversals, but the long-term direction of the change remains consistent. Unfortunately, the pace of change is slow relative to needs. Thus, one can still safely predict that, if we all come together a decade or two hence to discuss patterns of prejudice, there will be plenty of new evidence of the propensity of Americans to organize to suppress others because of their racial, religious, or ethnic traits.

There is, of course, the additional problem posed by race. The fact that race is such a visible characteristic, the fact that Negroes cannot become physically indistinguishable from other Americans simply by virtue of changes in their educational and occupational status—this undoubtedly means that racial prejudice is going to be much more difficult to eradicate than religious or ethnic prejudices. But one observation about political institutions can give us some encouragement: the political system not only functions as an arena within which religious or racial tensions can be expressed; it also serves as the avenue through which minority groups have gained first symbolic and later real power and status. Parties have nominated and elected members of minority groups that have been disliked by the great majority in order to gain the votes of the minority. As Gunnar Myrdal pointed out a quarter of a century ago, many politicians who are personally prejudiced often have supported measures fostering equality. Electing blacks to high office is an excellent way to improve the status of a group traditionally stereotyped as lowly. Hence, in addition to measures directly concerned with improving the educational and economic situations of the black population, it is important that both major parties be pressed to nominate and help elect black leaders. In this way, a new and much more hopeful chapter can be written in the doleful history of politics and prejudice.

As a final note on the politics of prejudice, it is important to recognize that right-wing political protest in America has almost invariably taken on an anti-elitist and often specifically anti-intellectual cast. In spite of the fact that such movements are seeking to preserve existing privileges and traditional values, they reflect the deep commitment to egalitarianism and the concomitant anti-elitism inherent in the American value system. When bigoted movements attacked Catholics and Jews in the past, they did so in part by identifying these groups with positions of political, economic, and cultural power. The Catholic danger to America was supposedly a result of a deliberate conspiracy by the Catholic hierarchy and the Pope, in league with Catholic politicians, to take over America and subject it to their European elitist structure and values. The Jewish threat was identified with the dire activities of international bankers. Even Communism must be presented as a threat flowing from within the elite, not from the poor. And when ethnic elites have not been available as a target, the focus of hostility has been directed against the Illuminati as the surrogate for the intellectuals.

The current upsurge of anti-intellectualism expressed by the Wallace movement has repeated the oldest populist American conspiracy theme, that which identifies changes in values and institutions with the deliberate subversive efforts of the intellectual elite. The Negroes, on the other hand, cannot and are not identified as part of the elite. They, therefore, are not the real villains; rather they are perceived as pawns manipulated by the Illuminati, the Communists, or the intellectuals, to achieve their subversive ends. Those involved in anti–civil rights movements can, therefore, honestly feel that they are not racists, that they are not anti-Negro. They can believe that the poor Negro who seeks to move out of the ghetto, who desires to put his child in an integrated school, who presses on white unions for membership, is only a weak tool, more to be pitied than hated. That the Birch Society, the Christian Crusade, or the American Independent Party, focus their resentments on intellectuals rather than Negroes, does not make the situation of the Negroes any better. It does point up, however, how the stress on racial and religious bigotry in America may paradoxically appear to decline at the same time that extremist movements designed to protect white supremacy and fundamentalist values are fostered. For such movements to succeed in America, the enemy must always be associated with the elite, never with the common man, whether he be black or white. As we have noted at the beginning, this anti-elitism is itself a form of prejudice, and, furthermore, it serves to mask the real and ultimate victims of bigotry.

Appendix to Chapter Two

Bibliographical Note

This article is based on research in process for a comprehensive book on the American radical right in historical perspective by Earl Raab and myself, which hopefully should appear in print published by Harper & Row in 1969. The detailed sources, both published and unpublished, for many of the statements presented here will be found in this forthcoming volume. Both this article and the larger book lean heavily on the theoretical approach for the study of mass movements presented in Neil Smelser, *A Theory of Collective Behavior* (New York: Free Press of Glencoe, 1963). Various of my previous writings deal with ideas and substantive work presented here. These include: Chapters 4, "Working-Class Authoritarianism," and 5, " 'Fascism'—Left, Right, and Center," in *Political Man* (Garden City: Doubleday, 1960), pp. 97–178; two articles, "The Sources of the Radical Right," and "Three Decades of the Radical Right: Coughlinites, McCarthyites, and Birchers," in Daniel Bell, ed., *The Radical Right* (Garden City: Doubleday, 1963), pp. 259–377; chapter 9, "Party Systems and the Representation of Social Groups," in *The First New Nation* (Garden City: Doubleday-Anchor, 1967), pp. 327–65; chapters 2, 5, 8 and 9, "Revolution and Counterrevolution: The United States and Canada," "Class, Politics, and Religion on Modern Society: The Dilemma of the Conservatives," "Religion and Politics in the American Past and Present," and "The Right-wing Revival and the 'Backlash' in the United States," in *Revolution and Counterrevolution* (New York: Basic Books, 1968), pp. 31–63, 159–76, 246–332; "On the Politics of Conscience and Extreme Commitment," *Encounter*, XXXI (August, 1968), 66–71; "George Wallace and the U.S. New Right," *New Society*, XII (October 3, 1968), 477–83; "Why Cops Hate Liberals—and Vice Versa," *The Atlantic*, CCIII (March, 1969), 76–83.

Some of the literature which pertains to the movements discussed here may be found in a variety of published works, as well as in Masters' essays and Doctoral dissertations.

GENERAL HISTORICAL WORKS

Ray Allen Billington, *The Protestant Crusade 1800–1860* (New York: Rinehart and Company, 1938); John Higham, *Strangers in the Land: Pattern of American Nativism 1860–1925* (New York: Atheneum, 1963); Gustavus Myers, *History of Bigotry in the United States* (New York: Capricorn Books, 1960); Edward J. Richter and Berton Dulce, *Religion and the Presidency* (New York: Macmillan, 1962); Richard Hofstadter, *Anti-Intellectualism in American Life* (New York: Alfred A. Knopf, 1963).

THE ANTI-ILLUMINATI AGITATION AND THE ANTI-MASONIC PARTY

Richard Hofstadter, *The Paranoid Style in American Politics* (New York: Alfred A. Knopf, 1965), esp. pp. 3–40; Vernon Stauffer, *New England and the Bavarian Illuminati* (New York: Columbia University Press, 1918); John Robison, *Proofs of a Conspiracy* (Boston, Western Islands, 1967, first published in 1798); David Brion Davis, "Some Themes of Counter-Subversion: An Analysis of Anti-Masonic, Anti-Catholic and Anti-Mormon Literature," *Mississippi Valley Historical Review*, XLVII (September, 1960), 205–24; Charles McCarthy, "The Anti-Masonic Party: A Study of Anti-Masonry in the United States, 1827–1840," *Annual Report of the American Historical Association for the Year 1902*, Vol. I (Washington, D.C.: Government Printing Office, 1903); Leland M. Griffin, "The Anti-Masonic Movement, 1826–1838" (Ph.D. Thesis: Department of Speech, Cornell University, 1950): Lorman A. Ratner, "Anti-Masonry in New York State" (M.A. Thesis: Department of Government, Cornell University, 1958); George H. Blakeslee, "The History of the Anti-Masonic Party" (Ph.D. Thesis: Department of History, Harvard University, 1903).

NATIVIST AND ANTI-CATHOLIC MOVEMENTS BEFORE THE CIVIL WAR

Ray Allen Billington, *op. cit.;* L. D. Scisco, *Political Nativism in New York State* (New York: Columbia University Press, 1901); Lee Benson, *The Concept of Jacksonian Democracy* (Princeton: Princeton University Press, 1961); Lawrence F. Schmeckebier, *History of the Know-Nothing Party in Maryland* (Baltimore: Johns Hopkins Press, 1899); John R. Mulkern, "The Know-Nothing Party in Massachusetts (Ph.D. Thesis: Department of History, Boston University, 1963); Robert D. Parmet, "The Know-Nothings in Connecticut" (Ph.D. Thesis: Department of History, Columbia University, 1966); William G. Bean, "Party Transformation in Massachusetts with Special Reference to the Antecedents of Republicanism" (Ph.D. Thesis: Department of History, Harvard

University, 1922); Leon D. Soule, "The Know-Nothing Party in New Orleans: A Reappraisal" (Ph.D. Thesis: Department of History, Tulane University, 1960).

NATIVIST AND ANTI-CATHOLIC MOVEMENTS IN THE LATTER PART OF THE NINETEENTH CENTURY

John Higham, *op. cit.;* Charles L. Sewrey, "The Alleged 'Un-Americanism' of the Church as a Factor in Anti-Catholicism in the United States, 1860–1914" (Ph.D. Thesis: University of Minnesota, 1955); Alvin P. Stauffer, "Anti-Catholicism in American Politics, 1865–1900" (Ph.D. Thesis: Department of History, Harvard University, 1933); Donald L. Kinzer, *An Episode in Anti-Catholicism: The American Protective Association* (Seattle: University of Washington Press, 1964); Irwin Unger, *The Greenback Era* (Princeton: Princeton University Press, 1964); Humphrey J. Desmond, *The APA Movement* (Washington: New Century Press, 1912); Priscilla F. Knuth, "Nativism in California, 1886–1897" (M.A. Thesis: Department of History, University of California, Berkeley, 1947).

BIGOTRY IN THE FIRST THREE DECADES OF THE TWENTIETH CENTURY

John Higham, *op. cit.;* Oscar Handlin, "American Views of the Jew at the Opening of the Twentieth Century," *American Jewish Historical Society,* XL (1951), 323–44; C. Vann Woodward, *Tom Watson: Agrarian Rebel* (New York: Oxford University Press, 1963); Leonard Dinnerstein, *The Leo Frank Case* (New York: Columbia University Press, 1968); David M. Chalmers, *Hooded Americanism: First Century of the Ku Klux Klan, 1865 to the Present* (Garden City: Doubleday, 1965); Arnold Rice, *The Ku Klux Klan in American Politics* (Washington, D.C.: Public Affairs Press, 1962); Jonathan N. Leonard, *The Tragedy of Henry Ford* (New York: G. P. Putnam's Sons, 1922); William Preston, Jr., *Aliens and Dissenters: Federal Suppression of Radicals 1903–1933* (Cambridge: Harvard University Press, 1963); John Mecklin, *The Ku Klux Klan* (New York: Harcourt Brace, 1924) ; Emerson Loucks, *The Ku Klux Klan in Pennsylvania* (Harrisburg: Telegraph Press, 1936); Charles C. Alexander, *The Ku Klux Klan in the Southwest* (Lexington: University of Kentucky Press, 1965); Gordon W. Davidson, "Henry Ford: The Formation and Course of a Public Figure" (Ph.D. Thesis: Department of History, Columbia University, 1966); David L. Lewis, "Henry Ford: A Study in Public Relations" (Ph.D. Thesis: Department of History, University of Michigan, 1959); Carey McWilliams, *A Mask for Privilege: Anti-Semitism in America* (Boston: Little, Brown and Co., 1948); Kenneth T. Jackson, *The Ku Klux Klan in the City* (New York:

Oxford University Press, 1967); Benjamin H. Avin, "The Ku Klux Klan, 1915–1925" (Ph.D. Thesis: Georgetown University, 1952); Kenneth E. Harrell, "The Ku Klux Klan in Louisiana" (Ph.D. Thesis: Louisiana State University, 1966); John A. Davis, "The Ku Klux Klan in Indiana, 1920–1930" (Ph.D. Thesis: Department of History, Northwestern University, 1966); Norman F. Weaver, "The Knights of the Ku Klux Klan in Wisconsin, Indiana, Ohio and Michigan" (Ph.D. Thesis: Department of History, University of Wisconsin, 1954); William P. Randel, *The Ku Klux Klan* (Philadelphia: Chilton Books, 1965).

THE EXTREMISMS OF THE 1930's

Morris Janowitz, "Black Legions on the March," in Daniel Aaron, ed., *America in Crisis* (New York: Alfred Knopf, 1951), pp. 305–25; Morris Schonbach, "Native Fascism During the 1930's and 1940's" (Ph.D. Thesis: UCLA, 1958); Marie Ann Buitrage, "A Study of the Political Ideas and Activities of Gerald B. Winrod" (M.A. Thesis: Department of Political Science, University of Kansas, 1955); Ralph Roy, *Apostles of Discord* (Boston: Beacon Press, 1953); Donald S. Strong, *Organized Anti-Semitism in America* (Washington, D.C.: American Council on Public Affairs, 1941); Victor C. Ferkiss, "The Political and Economic Philosophy of American Fascism" (Ph.D. Thesis: Department of Political Science, University of Chicago, 1954); David H. Bennett, "The Demagogues' Appeal in the Depression. The Origins and Activities of the Union Party: 1932–1936" (Ph.D. Thesis: Department of History, University of Chicago, 1963); Charles J. Tull, *Father Coughlin and the New Deal* (Syracuse: Syracuse University Press, 1965); Nick A. Masters, "Father Coughlin and Social Justice" (Ph.D. Thesis: Department of Political Science, University of Michigan, 1955).

THE RADICAL RIGHT IN THE POSTWAR ERA

Edward Shils, *The Torment of Secrecy* (Glencoe: The Free Press, 1956); Daniel Bell, ed., *The Radical Right* (Garden City: Doubleday, 1963); Michael P. Rogin, *The Intellectuals and McCarthy: The Radical Specter* (Cambridge: MIT Press, 1967); Jack Anderson and Ronald W. May, *McCarthy the Man, the Senator, the Ism* (Boston: Beacon Press, 1952); Reinhard H. Luthin, *American Demagogues* (Boston: Beacon Press, 1954) ; James Rorty and Moshe Dechter, *McCarthy and the Communists* (Boston: The Beacon Press, 1954); Richard Rovere, *Senator Joseph McCarthy* (New York: Meridian Books, 1960); Nelson W. Polsby, "Towards an Explanation of McCarthyism," *Political Studies*, VIII (October, 1960), 250–71; Martin Trow, "Small Businessmen, Political Intolerance and Support for McCarthy," *American Journal of Sociology*, LXIV

(November, 1958), 270–81; William R. McPherson, "Parallels in Extremist Ideology" (Ph.D. Thesis: Department of Social Relations, Harvard University, 1967); Burton Levy, "Profile of the American Right: A Case Study of Michigan" (Ph.D. Thesis: Department of Political Science, University of Massachusetts, 1966); Fred Grupp, "A Study of the Membership of the John Birch Society and the Americans for Democratic Action" (Ph.D. Thesis: Department of Political Science, University of Pennsylvania, 1968); J. Allen Broyles, *The John Birch Society* (Boston: Beacon Press, 1966); Benjamin Epstein and Arnold Forster, *The Radical Right, Report on the John Birch Society and its Allies* (New York: Vintage Books, 1967); Ira Rohter, "Radical Rightists: An Empirical Test" (Ph.D. Thesis: Department of Political Science, Michigan State University, 1967); Brooks H. Walker, *The Christian Fright Peddlers* (Garden City: Doubleday, 1964).

THREE

PREJUDICE AND THE CHURCHES

RODNEY STARK
and
CHARLES Y. GLOCK

Virtually every clergyman in America would agree that authentic religious commitment precludes racial and religious prejudice. But despite such unanimity, it is not at all clear what role religious convictions and religious institutions play in contemporary prejudice.

One is often tempted to accept the picture of the church suggested by the sight of priests, ministers, and nuns marching in Selma, Washington, and Chicago, or by the claims that clergymen such as Milwaukee's Father James Groppi are the vanguard of a "new breed" of Christians who are leading a crusade against sin, defined in social rather than personal terms.

But despite all these signs, one must not assume too readily that religion is always a powerful and reliable force against prejudice. For there are many discrepant indications that must also be considered. Indeed, clergymen have been forced from parishes for expressing even moderate views on racial and religious prejudice. And for every Father Groppi there always seems to be another clergyman who is willing to lead a counterdemonstration. For every minister who speaks out against prejudice there are a number of others who either do not want to get involved or fear that to do so would upset the laity. Furthermore, while it is obvious that many Christians are moved by their faith to regard all men as brothers, it is equally obvious that the majority of those who throw rocks at Negro marchers, who picket schools to prevent integration, or who become agitated about keeping Jews off their local school boards or out of their clubs, regard themselves as Christians. What is one to make of these contradictions?

This paper attempts to bring together what we have learned about the role of religion in contemporary prejudice from the Berkeley research program[1] and from similar studies of prejudice. First, the extent to which prejudice exists within the churches is assessed. The specifically religious factors that give rise to prejudice or that tend to reduce it are then considered. Finally, a few reflections are offered on what the churches can do. (Because of the limits of available data, we shall confine our attention to American Christian denominations.)

The Incidence of Prejudice

How much prejudice exists within the churches? The answer to this question depends very much on the level at which the churches are examined: at the official, or bureaucratic, level; among the general clergy; or at the level of the laity. At each level, it is important to assess religious prejudice, that is, prejudice against persons of other faiths or denominations; racial prejudice; and, finally, the view of the role of the churches in combatting prejudice.

[1] The University of California Five Year Research Program on Patterns of American Prejudice was supported by a $500,000 grant from the Anti-Defamation League of B'nai B'rith. Initial findings on the role of religion in prejudice have appeared in Charles Y. Glock and Rodney Stark, *Christian Beliefs and Anti-Semitism* (New York: Harper and Row, 1966), and in Gary T. Marx, *Protest and Prejudice* (New York: Harper and Row, 1967), Chap. 4.

THE OFFICIAL CHURCHES

At the official level of churches—i.e., the national bureaucratic and organizational apparatus, consisting of church leaders, commissions, agencies, governing bodies, councils of bishops, and the like—there is virtual unanimity: nearly all the major denominations have spoken out forcefully and repeatedly against prejudice, both religious and racial. In the area of religious prejudice, all major denominations are officially opposed to anti-Semitism. Furthermore, while the recent Vatican Council statement condemning the widespread belief that Jews are collectively guilty for the Crucifixion received considerable publicity, similar statements had been made a good deal earlier by most American Protestant bodies. Indeed, at the present time only the Lutheran Missouri Synod and the Southern Baptists seem to be having difficulty taking this position officially. On religious prejudice against other non-Christian groups, the churches have been less specific, but there is a growing moral sensitivity. At its 1968 national convention, for example, the Lutheran Church in America adopted a position on religious liberty which explicitly includes atheists and agnostics.

On matters of racial prejudice, the churches have been even more unanimous and outspoken. All major denominations have issued sharp condemnations of racial prejudice and specifically opposed discrimination in schooling, housing, and jobs. In addition to noble words, church bodies have also done some impressive deeds—from rewriting Sunday school and devotional materials to developing agencies devoted to action to oppose prejudice and discrimination.

THE CLERGY

When we look behind the superstructure of the churches and consider the views of the entire clergy rather than only those of religious leaders, we must make some important qualifications to the picture we have just sketched. If the official churches unanimously denounce prejudice and are committed to an active role in opposing it, the clergy as a whole are not unanimous on these same matters. It is unfortunate, but surely not surprising, to discover that a substantial minority of the clergy displays religious and racial prejudice.[2] Furthermore, even among unprejudiced clergymen there is a minority that does not believe the church ought to take an active role in the struggle for brotherhood. Nevertheless, the majority have relatively enlightened attitudes toward persons of other religions and races and do support the official actions of the churches. To give substance to these general remarks, let us consider some relevant research findings.

As already mentioned, officially the churches denounced the notion of collective and continuing Jewish guilt for the Crucifixion. The majority of the clergy support the official denunciations, but a minority continue to accept even the extreme forms of these notions. A recent national study of Protestant clergymen, conducted by Jeffrey K. Hadden, revealed that 6 per cent of the Methodist, 7 per cent of the Presbyterian, 21 per cent of the American Lutheran, 22 per cent of the American Baptist, and 38 per cent of the Missouri Synod Lutheran clergymen in his sample agreed with the statement that "The reason Jews have so much trouble is because God is punishing them for rejecting Jesus."[3]

As with attitudes toward Jews, clerical attitudes toward blacks are also mixed. Again, however, what data there are reveal that the majority of Christian clergy have fairly enlightened attitudes. For example, 80 per cent of the Protes-

---

[2] See Jeffrey K. Hadden, *The Gathering Storm in the Churches* (Garden City, N.Y.: Doubleday, 1969).

[3] Hadden, *op. cit.*

tant ministers in the Hadden study rejected the statement that "Negroes could solve many of their own problems if they were not so irresponsible and carefree about life," and only about one in ten opposed the civil rights movement. Among Roman Catholic diocesan priests, also about 10 per cent disapprove of the civil rights movement, according to Joseph Fichters' recent study of America's priests.[4]

The clergy, by and large, also supports an active role for the church in the struggle against discrimination. Here again one finds a minority that denies that the church has any business trying to reform society. However, a substantial majority does support an activist role for the churches and the clergy.

More than 75 per cent of the Protestant clergy in Hadden's samples agreed that "For the most part, the churches have been woefully inadequate in facing up to the civil rights issues." Similarly, large majorities favored direct action by the churches on social and moral issues. Indeed, nearly 80 per cent felt that if the church did not speak out on such matters, its very existence would be threatened. When direct action on the part of clergymen to protest racial injustice was considered, the clerical support was somewhat diminished. Still, a strong majority were in favor. As would be expected, such support declined considerably among Southern clergy and among clergy in conservative denominations such as the Missouri Synod.

Although somewhat marred, the picture that emerges from an examination both of church pronouncements on prejudice and of clerical attitudes is a hopeful one. It would appear that the churches ought to be able to play a significant role in the struggle against prejudice.

---

[4] See Joseph Fichters, *America's Forgotten Priests: What They Are Saying* (New York: Harper & Row, 1968).

THE LAITY

When we turn to rank-and-file church members, we get an entirely different perspective. The facts are that Christian laymen, as a group, are a rather prejudiced lot. It is perfectly obvious that large numbers of people in the churches, for whom Christian ethics provide an important basis for love, understanding, and compassion, are not prejudiced. But the majority of church members are prejudiced; furthermore, they deny the right of the churches to challenge their prejudices.

Looking first at religious prejudice, the following picture emerges: from half to two-thirds of American Christians would deny civil liberties to a person who does not believe in God. They would bar him from holding public office and remove him from a teaching position in the public schools. Similarly, half of American Christians continue to blame the Jews for the Crucifixion despite official pronouncements to the contrary. Worse yet, 33 per cent of American Christians score high and another 40 per cent score medium-high on an index made up of strongly anti-Semitic statements.[5]

Religious prejudice varies from denomination to denomination. Catholics are a bit less prone to such prejudice than are Protestants, and conservative Protestant bodies are somewhat more prejudiced than liberal Protestant groups. Nevertheless, religious prejudice is sufficiently widespread among laymen in all Christian bodies to constitute an important problem.

Turning to racial prejudice, one sees no change in this depressing picture. Among white Protestant and Catholic church members in the San Francisco-Bay Area of California,

---

[5] For example, "Jewish boys were less likely than Christain boys to volunteer for service in the armed forces during the last war"; "Jews are more likely than Christians to cheat in business"; "Jews, in general, are inclined to be more loyal to Israel than to America." Glock and Stark, *op. cit.*, pp. 124, 202.

nearly half say they would move if several Negro families moved into their block. A third think Negroes are less intelligent; nearly half blame Communists and other radicals for racial tension.[6] These data were collected in 1963 before any of the riots. Undoubtedly things are worse today. Indeed, a recent national survey conducted by the National Opinion Research Center for Jeffrey Hadden, 1967, showed that 89 per cent of the Christian laity felt that Negroes ought to take advantage of the opportunities society offers them and quit their protesting. And sadly, too, only those who rarely or never attended church dropped significantly below this proportion.[7] By way of contrast, only a third of Protestant clergy would support this view of Negro protest.[8]

This brings us to a final point about the contemporary Christian church member. Not only does he differ sharply from the official church and the clergy on the matter of his prejudice, he strongly opposes the role being played by the churches in overcoming discrimination. Thus, 70 per cent of the laity in the Hadden study denounced clerical involvement in social issues, such as civil rights. Indeed, data from a variety of recent studies indicate that the majority of laymen want their church to tend to the private religious needs of its members and to stay out of such questions as peace, social justice, and human rights.[9]

6 Some of these findings appear in Glock and Stark, *op. cit.* A fuller treatment of religion and racial prejudice based on the same data will appear in Rodney Stark and Charles Y. Glock, *By Their Fruits: The Consequences of Religious Commitment* (Berkeley and Los Angeles: University of California Press, forthcoming).

7 See Hadden, *op. cit.*

8 See Hadden, *op. cit.*

9 See Earl R. Babbie, "A Religious Profile of Episcopal Churchwomen," *The Pacific Churchman* (January, 1967); Charles Y. Glock, Benjamin B. Ringer, and Earl R. Babbie, *To Comfort and To Challenge* (Berkeley and Los Angeles: University of California Press, 1967). Findings from the Berkeley project which also support this tendency among laymen will appear in Rodney Stark and Charles Y. Glock, *The Poor in Spirit; Sources of Religious Commitment* (Berkeley and Los Angeles: University of California Press, forthcoming).

It is obvious that what one decides about the role of the churches in the battle against prejudice depends greatly on the level at which he examines the churches. For a moment let us think of the churches as a system having three parts. If we think of the official level as formulating the intentions of the churches, and the clergy as the means for achieving these intentions, it follows that the laity are supposed to exhibit the fruit of these intentions. But it is clear that although the intentions and the means are there, the intended consequences have not been forthcoming. Most of the laity continue to bear ill-will toward other races and religions. They may claim to love their brothers, but they are very finicky about whom they will call "brother." Thus, the system by which the words of the official churches are supposed to be translated into the hearts of the laity simply fails to operate effectively. The critical question is: Why?

Religious Influences on Prejudice

It seems clear that many Christians are able to justify racial and religious prejudice despite the official opposition of the churches to which they adhere. Thus, one must ask if it is possible that the churches are perhaps unwittingly doing something that contributes to this ability to rationalize prejudice. And further, is there anything the churches can do to reduce prejudice among their adherents? These are the questions that will guide the remainder of our discussion.

Broadly speaking we are concerned with two classes of factors that influence prejudice among the laity. The first of these is theological, i.e., teaching and doctrine that bear upon racial and religious prejudice and, in some aspects, seem to promote prejudice while in others appear to provide the churches with powerful means for overcoming it. The second class is represented by institutional constraints. These are features of the organization of the churches that affect the power of religious leaders to influence the views of the laity.

THEOLOGICAL FACTORS

The idea that Christian beliefs may be a source of prejudice is likely to be rejected out of hand by theologians and churchmen. Their view of the faith rules out the possibility of such a connection. Nevertheless, there can be a link between theology and prejudice, especially as doctrine is comprehended in the pew. Interpretations of the faith that are widespread among laymen are often not conducive to tolerance; they serve, instead, as a supporting dynamic for prejudice. This is true of both religious and racial prejudice, although the theological elements active in the two types are sometimes different.

Examining first the prejudice of Christian laymen toward persons of other faiths, such as Jews or Hindus, or even between Catholics and Protestants, a significant theological buttress for such prejudice is what we have called particularism —the notion that only one's own religion is true and legitimate and that others are therefore false.[10] In contemporary Christianity, particularism continues to flourish in interpretations of the doctrines that Christ offers the only way to salvation and that to reject him is to be condemned to eternal damnation. Unless such notions are held with a degree of sophistication that seems beyond the capacity of many laymen, they readily support prejudice. If others are seen as committed to a false religion and thus condemned to hell, it is but a short step to seeing them as inferior and immoral. Indeed, a commonly held particularistic doctrine holds that only through Christian teachings is morality made possible. The greater the strength with which particularistic theo-

10 See Glock and Stark, *Christian Beliefs and Anti-Semitism.*

logical views are held by Christians, and the more narrowly they are defined, the greater the hostility Christians harbor toward persons they see as religious outsiders: for example, Jews, Hindus, Moslems, and, of course, atheists and agnostics. Indeed, particularism generates hatred between Catholics and Protestants, and even between some Protestant groups.

When particularism is combined with the belief that the Jews crucified Christ and thus called down on themselves a collective and eternal curse, Christians display considerable vulnerability to general anti-Semitic beliefs. A Christian who sees the Jews as religiously illegitimate finds it difficult to resist other negative images of Jews.

These days few, if any, theologians would advocate a narrow particularism that would deny all religious virtue to non-Christians, and so far as we know no church officially endorses such doctrines. Indeed, the statements on religious liberty issued by various churches in the past several years uniformly condemn intolerance toward persons of other faiths. Nevertheless, these actions have had little impact upon rank-and-file Christians. A great many laymen continue to find theological support for their religious prejudices in such doctrines as the necessity of accepting Christ in order to be saved. Many feel that persons who refuse to accept the glad tidings have only themselves to blame for subsequent misfortunes.

Turning from religious to racial prejudice, the part played by theology is not so obvious. Christian particularism, while a potent source of prejudice toward Jews and other non-Christians, does not generate prejudice toward Negroes. Negroes by and large are Christian and not susceptible to the charge of rejecting Christ. Nor is any other theological rationale for racial prejudice immediately apparent. For example, only a few extremists argue that racial inferiority and segregation are proper Christian views, basing their view on certain interpretations of passages in the Old Testament.

In our initial investigations we failed to detect any very important relationships between customary measures of religious commitment and the considerable racial prejudice of church members. We found a higher incidence of racial prejudice among those who held conservative theological views, and among those who participated in church activities, private devotions, and the like.[11] These relationships were weak, however, and did not reveal any theological factor that contributed significantly to racial prejudice. The evidence of widespread racial prejudice among professing and practicing Christians, however, and the opposition among parishioners to active church involvement in civil rights, seemed nevertheless to hint that a subtle theological factor might be at work despite appearances to the contrary. Thus, we pursued the matter. Our investigations[12] are still not complete but, briefly, here is what we have discovered so far:

Underlying traditional Christian thought is an image of man as a free actor, as essentially unfettered by social circumstances, free to choose and thus free to effect his own salvation.[13] This free-will conception of man has been central to the doctrines of sin and salvation. For only if man is totally free does it seem just to hold him responsible for his acts, to punish him for his sins, and to demand repentance. Correspondingly, to the extent that a man's destiny is fixed by external forces, to that extent the notion of guilt is unjust. It has been widely recognized that this conception of human nature has been a mainspring in the development of Western

11 See Stark and Glock, *By Their Fruits.*

12 These will appear in Stark and Glock, *By Their Fruits.*

13 Our initial discussion of free-will doctrines appeared in Charles Y. Glock and Rodney Stark, *Religion and Society in Tension* (Chicago: Rand McNally, 1965), Chap. 15.

civilization and has greatly influenced our attitudes on personal accountability and the ingredients of personal success. An image of man as free and responsible lies behind such notions as rugged individualism, the self-made man, and the justification of wealth on the basis of merit. In short, Christian thought and thus Western civilization are permeated with the idea that men are individually in control of, and responsible for, their own destinies. If I am really the "captain of my soul" and "the master of my fate," then I have no one but myself to thank or to blame for what happens to me.

In the modern world, of course, these radical notions of unfettered free will have been somewhat modified. Still, a great many persons adhere to them in relatively pristine form, and they serve as lenses through which these people view and judge the behavior of others. The significance of this for prejudice is that radical and traditional Christian images of man prompt those who hold them to put the blame for disadvantage upon the individuals who are disadvantaged. A radical free-will image of man makes for an inability to perceive the effect of those forces outside the individual which may utterly dominate his circumstances. Thus, efforts to change the condition of the disadvantaged through social reforms appear irrelevant at best. Instead, one is led to dismiss the misery of the disadvantaged as due to their own shortcomings.

In pursuing this line of thought in our empirical studies we found that such an image of man tends to prevail among more active Christian church members and is strongly reflected in their disproportionate commitment to conservative politics.

The results of our empirical analysis lend themselves to the following interpretation: a free-will image of man lies at the root of Christian prejudice toward Negroes and of negative attitudes toward the civil rights movement; it also underlies the rejection of programs underwritten by the church and the government to improve the situation of minorities. The simple fact seems to be that a great many church people, because they believe men are mainly in control of their individual destinies, think that Negroes are themselves largely to blame for their present misery. It is not that these Christians condone the social forces that deprive black people, but rather that they simply do not recognize the existence of such forces in the world. They do recognize that Negroes are collectively disadvantaged. But the conclusion that logically follows from their theology is that this disadvantage must be the result of a racial shortcoming. For how else can one explain such a widespread racial circumstance, if one sees the world in primarily individualistic terms?

The flavor of this perspective on reality is perhaps best conveyed by those who accept it. Here are several comments written at the end of our questionnaires by Christian church members who took part in one of our major studies.

These are the views of a Protestant dentist:

> When I see the pictures of the poverty of Negroes on the TV and in the press I feel as sorry as anyone. But I am more depressed by all the "social-engineering" schemes that are being proposed to improve the lot of Negroes and others. Not only will these schemes destroy our free-enterprise heritage, but they will take away the only chance for the Negroes to live better lives. They do nothing about the real problem. The Negro is lazy, and short-sighted. He does not save his money or work to the future. And this is the only way anyone ever betters himself. If we turn to socialism for the answer we will simply make it impossible for the Negro to ever be better off, because under socialism individual initiative is destroyed, not created. We will all live in slums. Will that make Negroes feel better?

A Catholic housewife wrote: "The Irish came to this country way after the Negro and had it just as tough. Today we have an Irish president of the United States. The difference is hard work and the blessings of religion."

To the extent that Christian theology and institutions support a radical view of individual freedom and accountability, their members can be expected to reject the very premises upon which the battle against prejudice and discrimination rests. For if the disadvantaged condition of minority groups is proof of their unworthiness, how can people be expected to support measures to help them? In the eyes of such Christian laymen the doctrines of the church and its efforts on behalf of human rights often seem contradictory.

As we shall see shortly, this seeming contradiction provides a source of conflict that appears to accelerate a growing alienation between the churches and the laity. Furthermore, the prevalence of such doctrines among black Christians similarly affects Negroes' definitions of their own circumstances. Gary Marx's recent study of militancy in the black community, one of the studies in the aforementioned research program on prejudice, revealed a strong negative correlation between religious commitment and the desire for social justice and equality.[14] The more committed a Negro was to Christian beliefs and institutions the readier he was to see the lowly condition of Negroes as self-inflicted. Indeed, two-thirds of the urban Negroes in Marx's samples agreed that "Negroes who want to work hard can get ahead just as easily as anyone else," and about half agreed that "Before Negroes are given equal rights, they have to show that they deserve them."

Our analysis showed that the conception of man as wholly free was related to racial prejudice, but it was even more

14 See Gary T. Marx, *op. cit.*

closely related to opposing social action to improve the lot of disadvantaged minorities. Most lay opposition to church and clerical participation in human rights activities stems from the conviction that people get what they deserve in this life and the next.

A second interpretation of Christian doctrine that reinforces opposition to efforts to improve the lot of the disadvantaged is what we call the "miracle motif." This is the belief, most prevalent among evangelical Protestants, that if all men are brought to Christ, social evils will disappear through the miraculous regeneration of the individual by the Holy Spirit.

Billy Graham exemplifies this theological posture in his response to the social evils of our day. Recently, in answering critics' charges of indifference, Graham claimed to be a revolutionary. He argued that far from being unresponsive to the growing crises in human affairs—war, annihilation, inequality, hatred, and despair—he is actively pursuing a complete reconstruction of society. He claimed that he differs with his critics primarily on means, not ends. For Graham, the means are a miraculous revolution through individual salvation.

The perhaps unintended consequence of a preoccupation with individual salvation is a suspicion of, and often a hostility to, social and political efforts for reform. So long as there are men who have not been won to Christ, a sinful society is inevitable. Therefore, any attempts to reform society that do not require conversion to Christ are doomed to failure.

The power of Christian faith to transform individual lives is evidenced by Christian saints and martyrs of the past and present. There is less evidence, however, that faith applies wholesale and that the vast body of persons calling themselves

Christians have been so transformed. Nonetheless, individual conversion is the orientation which many Christians feel the church should take in confronting the problems of secular society.

This view is highly consistent with a free-will image of man. Indeed, like those who see man as in control of his own destiny, those for whom individual salvation is the key to social reform are prone to close their eyes to social factors that affect the individual. They hold that man chooses social disadvantage, social disadvantage does not choose man.

Beyond the notion that social change comes only through individual salvation, the miracle motif has broader implications for social reform. For a great many religious people, God is an active agent in worldly affairs. He ordains certain arrangements, sends certain tests, and in His own time brings about deliverance. We typically associate the fatalism inherent in this view with Eastern faiths, but it is not uncommon in Christianity. As a consequence, many people who might otherwise support or even help bring about changes, wait for God to do it. In his study of the black community, Gary Marx uncovered a strong vein of such sentiment.[15] About a third of Northern urban Negroes and more than half of Southern urban Negroes agreed that "Negroes should spend more time praying and less time demonstrating." One Negro clergyman interviewed in Marx's study said, "Praying is demonstrating." Another said, "I believe that if we all were pure . . . as we ought to be, there would be no struggle. When Peter was up, did the people march to free him? No. He prayed, and God did something about it."

Clearly, it is not only blacks who take this view. In a recent study of Episcopalian parishioners, it was found that when asked what the church could do to oppose war, a two

15 Marx, *op. cit.*

to one majority proposed purely religious means such as increased missionary activity or prayer.[16]

When the expectation of divine intervention becomes the sole response of many Christians to the problems of this world, it impedes the adoption of this-worldly solutions. The churches themselves do not officially hold that Christians should totally rely upon prayer as a means for social reform. And the very Christians who advocate waiting for God to solve the problems of discrimination would think a man insane who, wanting to learn algebra, only prayed and never studied. Thus, one wonders if there isn't a certain hypocrisy in the ease with which some Christians prescribe prayer and individual salvation as the answer to the immediate problems of discrimination. One is reminded of the young Negro who said, "Man, I've had that praying jazz. We prayed for 400 years. God helps him who helps himself."

Thus far we have concentrated on theological factors that seem to foster prejudice. Obviously this would be an extremely biased assessment if we did not also give attention to the capacities of theology to serve as a bulwark against prejudice. Christian claims about the stimulus for brotherhood, compassion, and love provided by the teachings of Christ are hardly partisan distortions. Rather, the ethical and moral teachings of the New Testament are rightfully used as a basis for all official church pronouncements on brotherhood. In our culture, such central ethical notions as "Love thy neighbor" and "Do unto others . . ." are pre-eminently religious teachings. Consequently we have also investigated the power of commitment to Christian ethics as a bulwark against prejudice, both religious and racial. Our findings produce an ironic contradiction, a basis both for future hope and for present disillusion.

16 See Glock, Ringer, and Babbie, *op. cit.*

First of all we find that as one might both hope and expect, individual commitment to Christian ethics provides a powerful antidote for prejudice. Persons high on ethical commitment are much less likely than others to hold religious and racial prejudices. *But the contradiction arises from equally persuasive evidence that commitment to Christian ethics is not related to other forms of Christian commitment.* Thus, while the ethics taught by the churches are a potent weapon against prejudice, it is not at all clear that the churches can claim direct credit for this fact. Instead, we found that those church members who accepted the other doctrines of the church, or who more regularly attended church or participated in church activities, were somewhat less likely to accept Christian ethics than those who were less orthodox in their beliefs and less regular in their participation.[17] That is to say, *Christians who are somewhat poorer church members judged on other criteria were more likely to be committed to the ethical teachings of the New Testament than were those who were otherwise better and more active members.* Thus, one is faced with the fact that Christian ethics is a powerful weapon against prejudice, but it is not clear that the churches are presently playing an important role in wielding this weapon.

We must emphasize that a great many devout Christians do accept Christian ethical teachings and are undoubtedly thereby inspired in their resolve to oppose prejudice. One need not look far to find many splendid examples. But when the whole range of Christians is examined, ethical commitment is, seemingly, not the typical product of religious devotion. When the churches search for support for their ethical teachings they are slightly more likely to find it among their

[17] See Rodney Stark and Charles Y. Glock, *American Piety: The Nature of Religious Commitment* (Berkeley and Los Angeles: University of California Press, 1968).

most dormant members than they are to find it among the most active. Thus, the churches have not been effective in getting ethical doctrines across.

In addition to Christian ethics, a final doctrinal consideration is what we call the "moral cliché." Moral clichés are statements of high principle that are nearly unanimously agreed to but that people fail to manifest in concrete behavior. Let us consider some examples. Ninety-one per cent of both Catholic and Protestant church members in our California samples agreed with the statement "Love thy neighbor means that we should treat all races the same." Virtually identical proportions also agreed that "Negroes ought to have the same rights and opportunities as others." Such unanimous sentiments certainly seem promising for the future of race relations. But despite having proclaimed their Christian love and advocated equal rights for Negroes, these people contradict themselves as soon as they are asked to make concrete applications. On the very page of the questionnaire on which the overwhelming majority professed their commitment to Christian brotherhood in principle, more than 40 per cent of these same Christians said they would move if several Negro families came to live on their block, and nearly a third said they did not want to have Negroes in their churches.[18]

This discrepancy between principle and behavior illustrates a major difficulty in the role of the churches in combatting discrimination. It does little good for men to hold high principles if they are unable to recognize when and how these principles relate to their affairs. The failure of the churches is partly reflected in this inability. Often the churches are not really in a position to draw out the concrete implications of the high principles they teach. Instead they often seem to feel they must settle for teaching the abstract

[18] See Glock and Stark, *Christian Beliefs and Anti-Semitism.*

principles and hoping that parishioners will manage to see the implications on their own. We shall now try to say something about why this is so. What are some of the structural constraints that prevent the churches from translating their official intentions into demonstrations of Christian witness, especially among the laity?

Structural Constraints upon the Role of the Church

The central structural problem for the modern church is the question of authority. Generally speaking, it appears that often the church knows where it wants to lead, but as we have seen, it is often unable to do so.

Perhaps the most severe constraint upon the authority of the official church resides in the composition of its lay clientele: the factors that today best provide the churches with their members' commitment work against church authority, especially in dealing with social rather than personal problems. In a recent study of church members, the church has been characterized as having two main functions: the comforting and the challenging.[19] The comforting function is to provide persons with inner peace, with the ability to cope with their various existential anxieties. The challenging function, on the other hand, refers to efforts of the churches to exert moral leadership, to arouse members' interest in matters larger than themselves.

It was also suggested that there may be a certain inherent tension between these two functions of the churches, that persons whose religious commitment is grounded on the comforts of faith may be reluctant to accept the challenges of faith.

Research has borne out this suspicion. People who seek comfort for personal disappointments and anxieties through

[19] See Glock, Ringer, and Babbie, *op. cit.*

religion are opposed to those aspects of the churches that are devoted to a challenging function.[20] *But perhaps even more serious is the fact that comfort-seekers constitute the bulk of the most active Christian laity: it is their money and participation upon which contemporary Christian organizations rest. Thus, there is a built-in resistance to the challenge function in the churches.* Efforts to confront these people with challenges lead to conflict and often to rebellion. Thus, the churches risk the strongest base of their member support by being too active. A possible solution, of course, might be to rekindle the religious commitment of those who are concerned with questions of social justice. At the present time, however, the more a person is concerned with these matters the less active he is in the churches, the less he attends, and the less he contributes.[21]

Resistance to change by the comfort-seeking majority in the churches is not always passive. It is hardly a secret that a good many pastors around the nation have been forced to resign for speaking out strongly on problems of prejudice or for becoming involved in activities aimed at achieving social justice for minority groups. It has been reliably reported in the press that the Episcopal Church in California suffered serious declines in contributions following its strong opposition to Proposition 14, the measure that repealed the State's Fair Housing Law. Indeed, a catalog of such events would be extremely lengthy.[22]

A wide-ranging reaction of the clergy to such threats is timidity. Rather than risk a major outbreak in their congregations, pastors have been conspicuously absent from the ranks of clerical activists. For example, Jeffrey K. Hadden's

[20] See Glock, Ringer, and Babbie, *op. cit.;* Babbie, *op. cit.;* and Stark and Glock, *By Their Fruits.*
[21] See Stark and Glock, *American Piety.*
[22] See Hadden, *op. cit.*

several recent studies of ministerial participation in civil rights protest have shown that parish pastors rarely take part.[23] The activist clergy occupy positions in the churches that are not directly exposed to lay pressure, being heavily drawn from among denominational administrators, seminary faculties, chaplains, and the like. Hadden's studies showed that clergy who demonstrate do not differ from clergy who do not in terms of attitudes or theology but apparently only in their freedom to participate.

Obviously, the extent to which pastors are immediately vulnerable to a lay rebellion differs from denomination to denomination. The vulnerability is greatest when the laity are the pastor's employers, when they can simply fire him by voting to do so. Correspondingly, pastors are somewhat less vulnerable when they can only be removed by their bishop. Still, harmony in a congregation is highly prized, especially by bishops, and in the long run the whole church is vulnerable to widespread withholding of funds or affiliation.[24]

In this sense, the contemporary churches are held captive by a comfort-seeking laity who want their pastor to devote all his time to private religious needs. As a consequence, some of the seeming discontinuity between the pronouncements of the official church and the outlook of the laity stems from the reluctance of many pastors to preach the official position from the pulpit. When national conferences of church leaders meet and issue their pronouncements, they are made up mainly of men who are not directly vulnerable to member opposition. In fact, studies have shown that the majority of laymen never even find out what policies their leaders enunci-

---

23 Hadden, *op. cit.*, and Jeffrey K. Hadden and Raymond C. Rymph, "Social Structure and Civil Rights Involvements: A Case Study of Protestant Ministers," *Social Forces*, XLV, No. 1 (September, 1966), 51–61.

24 See, for example, Ernest Q. Campbell and Thomas F. Pettigrew, *Christians in Racial Crisis* (Washington, D.C.: Public Affairs Press, 1959).

ated.[25] Thus, admirable words are often spoken and deeds done with minimal risk. But when the risks are high, as in face-to-face confrontations with the laity, the actions are minimal. As constituted today, the churches do not have sufficient authority over their lay members greatly to alter their prejudiced views or even to speak too boldly about them unless they are willing to take some risks.

What Can Be Done?

In conclusion, we would like to give some attention to the implications we see in our findings for the future policy of the churches. We are not theologians, and many of these problems require considerable theological understanding. Nevertheless, one may find some general lessons here for prejudice reduction.

The first lesson, in our judgment, is that ideas are important social forces. There has been a tendency in our society, encouraged by social science, to regard the ideas men hold somehow as epiphenomena, as simply reflections of other variables such as social class and education, or of deeper psychological forces such as authoritarianism, anxiety, anomie, and the like. This tendency has been especially pronounced in regard to religious ideas. Even a good many churchmen have come to think that religious ideas play little part in the way men evaluate and act upon the world around them. It may well be true that religious ideas have little influence on some aspects of modern life. The main conclusions of our studies, however, is that theological notions and convictions play an important role in religious and racial prejudice. It matters greatly whether or not Christians hold particularistic conceptions of Christianity, blame the Jews for the Crucifixion, hold a radical free-will image of man, or on

25 See Glock, Ringer, and Babbie, *op. cit.*

the other hand are strongly committed to the ideals of Christian ethics. These beliefs considerably influence prejudice, quite independently of the effects of class, education, authoritarianism, anomie, and similar factors which have preoccupied social scientists.

If we accept the evidence that religious ideas are important in prejudice, we must then face the fact that at present they more commonly function to sustain prejudice than to overcome it. From this observation it follows that if the churches are morally committed to conquering prejudice, they must take theological issues seriously. We would pose the following as some central questions for theological consideration:

1. Do the churches mean for their adherents to believe that only Christians can be saved? How can doctrinal reformulations that are meant to provide religious legitimacy to non-Christians be stated simply so they can be widely understood and accepted?

2. Is a free-will image of man, as we have earlier described it, essential to contemporary Christian doctrine? If not, what can be done to supplant such notions, since they are widespread among both clergy and laity and play a powerful role in supporting prejudice?

3. Is contemporary Christianity really committed to the miracle motif in human affairs? How can the notions of an active God be more effectively made to harmonize with the need for direct human action?

4. How is it possible for persons who ardently proclaim their Christian orthodoxy to reject the doctrines of Christian ethics. Is this not heterodoxy? If so, is it not pertinent to suggest that ethical proclamations ought to be so inextricably implicated in confessions of faith and in true orthodoxy as taught by the churches that such a separation is no more possible than would be a belief in the divinity of Jesus but not in the existence of God? Could the churches undertake

emergency measures to give as much emphasis to the ethical demands of the faith as they do to its promise of salvation?

Speaking as nontheologians, we suspect that particularism, radical notions of free-will, and extreme "miracle motifs" are not essential to contemporary Christian thought. If this is so, then we believe it is crucial that the churches concentrate on convincing their members of this fact. By doing so they could make an extremely important contribution to reducing our capacities to hate one another.

Indeed, of all the major institutions in society, the churches may be in the best position to make deep inroads on contemporary prejudices. This is true partly because of past failures. For on Sunday morning those Americans who most need to have their prejudices shaken are more likely to be found in church than at home reading the newspapers or watching the football game of the week. But in addition, the church alone among society's institutions is specifically concerned with sin and righteousness. It is the avowed task of the churches to ask men the moral significance of their thoughts and actions.

This leads to our final consideration—the extent to which the churches can reasonably be expected to act on these suggestions. Although ideally the churches are primarily concerned with transcendent matters, they are also formal organizations subject to the mundane forces that bear upon all such organizations. Given the built-in constraints that oppose the authority and the ability of the churches to confront questions of prejudice, can we expect them to act more vigorously and effectively than they have? We cannot anticipate how the churches will take up this problem of authority. In the final analysis it seems likely that the course followed by the church will depend upon how it really sees itself and its mission.

If the church is willing to settle for being a successful organization, in terms of buildings and budgets, then perhaps it cannot really do more than it has. But if there is widespread conviction among churchmen that the Christian church is primarily a moral instrument, a unique servant of righteousness, then perhaps the churches will be willing to run some risks. Given the fact that it presently rests upon a disproportionately comfort-seeking base, the church will have to take some risks—including the risk of losing some members—in order to act. But by taking these risks the churches may be able to activate some of those presently dormant Christians who share the official views of what the churches ought to stand for. One way or another such measures would almost certainly cause some convulsions within the churches. But at this moment there are convulsions throughout our society. Dare the churches remain aloof?

FOUR

THE MASS MEDIA AND PREJUDICE[1]

DORE SCHARY

The mass media can affect prejudice and discrimination through their news reports and commentaries, through the content of their entertainment and public service programs, and in their hiring and promotion policies. Their behavior has important implications for the control of prejudice and discrimination in society, although the media are not always conscious of their role. In this chapter we shall explore the media's performance, consider how to improve it, and raise some issues about the media's acknowledged responsibility to serve the public interest.

Prejudice and the Reporting of News

Despite much heated discussion and controversy, very little is known about the effects on prejudice of the handling of news. The image that the media would like to project and that they work hard to achieve is of reporting of the news

1 This chapter is based on a discussion, The Mass Media and Prejudice, at the symposium Patterns of American Prejudice. Mr. Schary served as moderator of the panel; the participating communications experts included James Bassett, director of the editorial page, *Los Angeles Times;* Ernest Dunbar, senior editor, *Look Magazine;* Ben Holman, Department of Justice; William Kaland, director of program development, Westinghouse Broadcasting Company; and John F. White, president, National Educational Television.

objectively—in the jargon of the day, of "telling it like it is." Objectivity is presumably a standard to be upheld in all places at all times and under all circumstances. By and large, this commitment to objectivity is a criterion for news reporting about which everyone in a free society agrees. But in the midst of this general consensus, there is much disagreement about what being objective means and, therefore, about whether the media are being objective or not. This disagreement over how objectivity shall be understood and practiced is responsible for most of the controversies surrounding the media's treatment of minority groups that are the victims of prejudice—Negroes, Jews, Mexican-Americans, Puerto Ricans, American Indians. Problems arise from decisions both about what news to report and about how to report it.

NEWS SELECTION

It would seem offhand that deciding what news to report is not a matter of objectivity but one of editorial style, of newsworthiness, and of audience appeal. To be sure, a commitment to objectivity might require "equal time" for an opposing view when a news story reports one side of a controversy; but ordinarily news does not have this controversial character, and if a medium reports a story about a political event or a crime or an item of human interest accurately, its responsibility to be objective would seem to be fulfilled.

Actually the matter is not nearly so simple. When one examines the totality of news coverage, one soon sees that a newspaper, radio station, television station, or news magazine can be impartial in what it reports and at the same time highly biased in what it selects to report. Thus, a newspaper may meet the highest standard of objectivity in its reports about crimes in which black Americans are involved, but its editor may systematically ignore the black community in his choice of positive human-interest stories.

The mass media do not presently acknowledge an obligation to be objective in news selection, and their performance indicates that they are not. Ordinary selection procedures are likely on balance to present a negative picture of minority groups. This is not what the media consciously intend, though individual editors or reporters may wish it, but is due to certain built-in features of media operation. One of these features is the media's tendency to consider the sensational, the unusual, the deviant, and the lurid as newsworthy, while the ordinary, the commonplace, and the benign are not. The total effect of this policy is to produce a bleak view of the over-all human condition even without discriminating against some specific minority group.

To complicate the picture, because of past and present deprivation and oppression, minority groups are demonstrably more prone to deviant behavior, as this is defined by the dominant majority. Therefore they are more likely to be newsworthy by the media's standards. If white-collar crimes were detectable—padding expense accounts, fudging on tax returns, juggling books, taking bribes or payoffs—then the crime rate for whites might very well exceed that for Negroes. But, of course, such white-collar crime is not reported, with the result that the "deviant" behavior of the minority group is simply more visible than that of the majority.

The minority group member is penalized by news selection procedures not only because he is more likely to have negative news reported about him but also because he is less likely to have good news reported. One reason for this is that minority group members are insufficiently represented on news staffs, and it helps to be a member of a group to write a feature story about it. The white reporter, for example, no matter how unprejudiced, is not as likely to search out and find a positive human interest story about a black family as about a white one. Editors, like reporters, are usually selected from the majority group and are prone to see the world from a white perspective. So far only a few appear to have been sensitive enough to go out of their way to give a minority group a "fair shake" in news selection. Most continue to find the good news only in the majority community. Such preferences assure that black or brown or red men do not do the things that "count" and do not get positive stories written about them.

This imbalance appears considerable, however much it may have improved recently, and it seems to reinforce, if not to produce, prejudice. The media are still the only source of many people's images of minority groups and how are such people to know that the black American about whom they hear evil things is the exception and not the rule? No one expects that the mass media can overturn the results of years of oppression simply by modifying news selection procedures. In the long run, we are going to have to revise a great many practices of a great many institutions. But even just changing news selection procedures could, we believe, produce a significant improvement.

What are the alternatives for the media? One possibility, of course, is for them to continue their present practices on the grounds that the effects attributed to them have not been proven. The adoption of such a position would seem to put the burden of proof on the media—that is, they would be required to show whether or not these practices are justified. In the absence of such an effort, the media's denial of the charge of bias can only be viewed as a delaying tactic to ward off needed reform.

A second alternative is for the media to extend their commitment to objectivity in news reporting to apply to news selection as well—at least for news within the area of present concern. They would have to think, debate, and decide about what objectivity means in this context. A minimum requirement would include some effort on the media's part to insure that they do not convey false impressions about what minority groups are like by the way they select the news; a willingness to rethink and amend standards of newsworthiness so that they do not reflect so much the values and interests of the dominant majority; an attempt to balance negative stories about minority groups with positive ones; and a concerted drive to recruit and train much larger numbers of minority group members for news staffs. The media can rightfully claim that they are moving in most if not all these directions, but they must become much more conscious about what is going on in minority life and much more self-conscious about how to report it.

A third alternative for the media is to move beyond what may be a reasoned objectivity in news selection, though not in news reporting, and unabashedly enter the struggle against prejudice. This would call for the media to select news and commentary in such a way as to educate their audiences, to breed a kind of sophistication about prejudice that would enable an audience to recognize it in itself and to want to do something to eliminate it. In such a strategy news about these minority groups would be selected not by the old standards of newsworthiness but by new ones that would give priority to stories reporting the "positive ordinary" rather than the "negative extraordinary" in minority group life. News about Negro altruism, for example, would dominate over news about Negro crime. The stability as well as the instability of Negro families would be pointed out. Black workers would be revealed to be responsible, efficient, and hard working as white workers when they are treated as fairly. The media would undertake to explain why minority group males are not as frequently doctors, lawyers, scientists, and business executives. Within minority contexts, the achievements of persons in less elevated positions would have to be described for the accomplishments that they are.

Pursuing this alternative would in effect mean turning the whole machinery around so that the minority groups, instead of getting the short end of the news selection stick as they now do, would for a change be getting the long end. This kind of "compensatory" treatment would undoubtedly be difficult for many white editors and reporters and readers to accept. I am not necessarily recommending it. I am merely indicating it as one of several possible routes that the media might take in selecting news.

NEWS REPORTING

Objectivity in news presentation goes beyond news selection to include the treatment of the stories that are reported. Once again some choice is involved in deciding which details to report, and bias can enter into the decision-making process. Not only the actual words but the way a story is featured can influence the total impression. It probably makes a difference whether a newspaper story gets front-page or back-page treatment, what is said in the opening paragraphs, whether or not the story carries a byline, or whether pictures are used; if on radio or television, the prestige or popularity of the commentator can be important.

Given the number and variety of ingredients that make up a news story, objectivity is difficult both to define and to achieve. We tend to believe that newsmen are mostly free of prejudice, and, indeed, that they are more than usually sensitive and sympathetic toward its victims. But out-and-out prejudice is probably less threatening to objectivity in reporting than are other more subtle factors, such as the common practice of assigning stories concerning minorities to reporters

untrained in intergroup relations and recruited from the
majority group. Certain nuances of a group's life are unlikely
to be caught by untrained outsiders, no matter how honor-
able their intentions. As the report of the Kerner Commission puts it, "along with the country as a whole, the press
has too long basked in a white world, looking out of it, if at
all, with white men's eyes and a white perspective."

The Kerner Commission commended the news media for
achieving reasonable balance in their reporting of the summer disturbances in 1967. By statistically balancing the stories
treating the disturbances in different ways and from different points of view, the commission implied that the media
had not sensationalized the disturbances, not overplayed violence, and not given disproportionate time or space to extremist leaders. But when the commission study went on to
more qualitative findings, it noted that the media "printed
scare headlines unsupported by the mild stories that followed," "reported rumors that had no basis in fact," "staged
'riot' events for the cameras," "reported inaccurate information about the extent of the damage," and "tended to define
the events as black-white confrontations," even though "almost all of the deaths, injuries, and property damage occurred
in all-Negro neighborhoods." What is required is to gain a
sense of the effect on the audience of such reporting. Of this,
we know almost nothing, yet how people respond to the news
is as important as personnel practices, news selection, and
reporting procedures.

These observations imply that the media should seek to
recruit more minority group members on their news staff;
that newsmen assigned to cover stories about minorities be
trained in intergroup relations; that the media should be
sensitive to prejudice among their own staff. And, indeed, the
media, by and large, are already doing these things and are

sensitive, as the Kerner Commission has pointed out, to their responsibilities in the reporting of minority group news.[2] The most urgent unmet requirement at present is the knowledge of the actual consequences of different news procedures. We need to know what difference it makes when a Negro or white reporter is sent out to cover a specific disturbance; what impressions are conveyed to the public by the ways disturbances are reported. Does it help to have the media try to balance their reporting as they did in the summer of 1967, or does the public itself seek out, select, and remember the sensational and violent no matter how much counterinformation is supplied? What effects, if any, do the news and its mode of reporting have on prejudice?

Entertainment, Public Service, and Advertising

However hard it is to define and apply, objectivity serves as a standard for news reporting on which most observers and practitioners can agree. There is no similarly agreed upon principle in determining how minority groups are to be treated when the media are engaged in entertaining, providing public service, or selling. Perhaps a minimum requirement might be that the media should not sustain prejudiced views in their portrayal of minorities in films, documentaries, entertainment programs, fictionalized accounts, and advertis-

2 The good will of media executives is also demonstrated in a recent study by Woody Klein, "News, Media and Race Relations: A Self Portrait," *Columbia Journalism Review* (Fall, 1968), pp. 42–49. On the basis of a survey of executives of magazines, newspapers, and radio and television stations, Klein concludes: "The survey has shown that the media have become aware of shortcomings after decades of neglect. Like so many other professions, journalism is beginning to recognize its responsibility in the quest for better race relations in America. There are definite signs of progress. But only when coverage of Negroes in the United States, as well as stories about the relationship between blacks and whites, becomes an everyday phenomenon and not just a "special"—only then will this country have arrived at a point where prejudice will no longer exist in the mass media."

ing. But can we carry this position a step further and require that the media should be engaged actively in a struggle against prejudice? There are at least two different points of view on this issue. Some believe the media have the responsibility to work actively to bring about society's highest values. Others take a somewhat less stringent view, believing that the media are not designed to serve as society's conscience and guide, that it is not their responsibility actively to promote social values.

When we turn to what the media have actually done in these areas, we find a somewhat mixed record. They have provided some of the most eloquent testimonies to brotherhood and good will that we have known in our time. Yet overall their performance has fallen far short of what it could have been. While seized with crusading spirit from time to time, mostly they have accommodated themselves to reflecting the culture rather than leading it. Despite many hopeful signs, it is still possible that the media may unwittingly be nourishing prejudice.

With the benefit of hindsight we have learned to shudder at the way the American Negro has been portrayed in the past. Not long ago he was traditionally presented as servant or comedian—superstitious, cowardly, servile, obsequious, good-natured, and inferior. White writers, white producers, and white directors constructed black roles primarily to fit white stereotypes—"black boys" carrying white men's luggage, black natives sneaking around the jungle, black tap dancers doing a buck-and-wing.

Today, of course, such demeaning portrayals would not be tolerated by the media even in the South. Negroes now appear in roles that would have been unthinkable less than a decade ago. In television series, motion pictures, plays, short stories, and novels, largely written and produced by white men, blacks have come to be heroes. We have seen during the last five years a raft of superb documentaries on various aspects of Negro culture and history. Even advertising has felt the change as black faces mingle with white ones in newspaper ads and television commercials.

A remarkable change has occurred to be sure. But the culture too has changed, and while the media have transcended the past, it is not clear that they have also transcended the culture. Indeed, the media may be as unknowingly accommodating to today's prejudices as they were to the prejudices of the past. So, for example, just as our society is nearly silent on the subject of Mexican-Americans, Puerto Ricans, and American Indians, the media too are silent. By this silence the media obviously do not intend to condone prejudice against these groups. But such, of course, is the indirect result. For where prejudice is not directly engaged, it is in effect sustained.

Undoubtedly some progress has been made in the media's treatment of the black community. By virtue of their numbers and growing power the black minority is compelling the attention of the media today. But how is this attention paid and with what effect? Deciding how to treat the black man in this new age has been an enigma for the media. By and large media people want to help the cause of the black man. But how, they ask themselves, can this be done without upsetting the economic applecart or producing loud protests of unfair treatment from either the white community or the black? The media have tried various formulas. The one that has proven most successful represents an amazing turnabout of past performance. What we have seen happen in recent years is a transformation in the qualities attributed to the Negro—from everything the white man despises to, everything he admires. Thus, for fearful subservience and mindless good nature, we see substituted vitality and good looks, upward mobility and family stability, hard work and material success.

The media can point to exceptions to this portrait. Certainly there have been films—one thinks of *Nothing But a Man* and *One Potato, Two Potato*—which have depicted more tellingly and accurately what it means to be black in a white society. And documentaries rarely fall prey to this kind of reverse stereotyping. But the dominant portrait of the black man in the mass entertainments—motion pictures and television drama, variety and comedy shows and in advertising—is the simple-minded one. The message that comes across all too often is that blacks are fine provided they display the traditional white middle-class values. Sidney Poitier's recent roles on the screen, Bill Cosby's "I Spy" and most recently Diahann Carroll's in the new television series "Julie" exemplify the portrait, as do the young clean-cut and successful blacks who have increasingly begun to appear in ads and commercials.

Some whites would undoubtedly prefer to have Negroes, as other minority groups, ignored. But next best to not seeing the black man at all is seeing him in a light which reveals only white men's values. Thus, the media would seem to have found an expedient solution that does not apparently offend anyone. But is this reverse stereotyping really having the effect it was presumably intended to have—namely the reduction of prejudice? Can the white man be made less prejudiced by being shown that the black man is really a kind of carbon copy of himself? Is it possible that by showing mostly successful Negroes the old stereotype is being supported that all blacks can be successful if they only try? Doesn't the breakdown of prejudice require that the white man come to recognize and feel discomforted about what it really means to be black in a white society—to be rejected, to be hurt, to be treated as an object? And doesn't it require that we come to acknowledge and respect the real difference in values and life-style?

We simply do not know the answers to these questions. No study has been carried out. The public is amazingly complacent about the media's trying all sorts of strategies that might drastically affect the quality of social life without demanding to know what that effect might be. A pharmaceutical house cannot release a new drug on the market without first subjecting it to rigorous tests; yet the public evidently finds social illnesses far less threatening than physical illnesses, or it feels that social ills are just too big and too complex to be dealt with rationally. Until public pressure mounts, the media may continue to plead innocent until proved guilty.

Perhaps we would be less uneasy about the media's "black is white" formula if it were counterbalanced by a strong effort to tackle the prevention and cure of prejudice head on. In the previous generation, motion pictures such as *Pinky* and *Gentlemen's Agreement* represented breakthroughs for their time. Today prejudice is more often being dealt with explicitly and sensitively in motion pictures, plays, satires, and documentaries. A recent and distinguished case in point is the CBS television series "Of Black America." But such productions represent isolated events. No medium is attempting to drive home the message of tolerance persistently in programs that reach mass audiences. I am not necessarily suggesting that the media should do this, for perhaps such explicit education for tolerance might be resented by viewers or readers suspicious of being "brainwashed." But surely some of this problem can be avoided by presenting without preaching. In many cases the fact of deprivation and oppression will speak for themselves.

Personnel Policy and Practice

The key to solving many of the media's minority group problems is undoubtedly personnel. So long as the black American must rely on white editors, reporters, writers, producers, and directors to represent him, his life will undoubtedly be shown from a white perspective. Media people and media critics alike seem to agree on this point.

Like most other institutions, the media have had a history of discriminatory employment practices. As recently as a decade ago there was only a handful of Negro newsmen and editors and practically no Negro media executives. There were no blacks on the big hit shows, the quiz shows, or the soap operas, except in the traditional servant roles, and few in the technical end of the industry. A major breakthrough came in 1955 when Leontyne Price sang the title role in Puccini's *Tosca* on NBC, the first time a Negro had sung on a nationally televised opera broadcast. Since then the picture has gradually improved, but the pace has been painfully slow. In 1964, Jesse H. Walker, city editor of the *New York-Amsterdam News,* a black paper, was quoted as saying, "Television is growing as far as the image of the Negro is concerned. Still it has a long way to go." A survey by *TV Guide* in 1964 reported that not one Negro was then employed by a television network or station in a top executive or administrative post. At about the same time newspapers began searching for Negro reporters, but with such lack of success as to result in demonstrations and sit-ins by civil rights organizations against a number of the nation's leading newspapers.

Despite the sharply narrowing focus on the problems of minority Americans, the situation is not much better today than it was in 1964. Minority groups continue to be underrepresented in almost every aspect of media operations except for the more menial jobs. The aforementioned study by

Woody Klein reports that in 1968 5.1 per cent of magazine employees were Negro. The equivalent figures for newspapers and for radio-TV were 4.7 per cent and 2.7 per cent.[3] Attitudes have continued to improve, however, and the media now point out that they have more unfilled jobs for minority people than they have qualified people to fill them.

It is questionable, though, whether simply making more jobs available to Negroes is sufficient to alter the racial mixture of media staffs. For one thing these jobs are publicized pretty much as if the job-seeking practices of blacks were just like those of whites, when they are not. The inadvertent result is to discriminate against blacks who have not been educated to use the employment aids that the white community makes available. In addition, because many media executives have come to believe it is more difficult to fire a black man than a white man, especially from high level jobs, a black applicant may have to be even more qualified than his white counterpart.

Other common personnel practices that may discriminate are the reliance on personnel tests developed and standardized on white samples and the tendency to impose middle-class standards of dress, appearance, and deportment in evaluating job applicants. The preference for graduates of elite schools and colleges in professional recruitment drives also works against black applicants. Furthermore, many white men still find it hard to take orders from a black man, no matter what his qualifications. Personnel managers may therefore choose not to promote a qualified Negro, using the fear that he would not be effective in his new job to rationalize their actions.

To ensure that Negroes and other minority group members are not discriminated against in employment takes sen-

3 *Ibid.*

sitivity and courage. Even these qualities will not be enough unless management gives its unequivocal support. So far in the mass media—despite notable brave exceptions—neither the courage nor support has been consistently forthcoming.

Moreover, eliminating discrimination in hiring and promotion is only half the job. If blacks and whites were treated exactly equally today, the former would still be penalized because of the unfair treatment they have received in the past. Compensatory treatment is necessary over an extended period of time if equal opportunity is to become a reality, not just a slogan. Media executives, like other kinds of executives, probably approve this idea in principle and deny it in practice. It requires extraordinary perception and sympathy on the part of white Americans to acknowledge that for a time Negroes in America need more than a fair deal. Yet until this idea is taken seriously, progress in producing the equality everybody says they want is likely to be exceedingly slow. In a modest way the media have already begun to introduce some compensatory measures. They have provided special fellowships for minority students interested in media careers. They have set up on-the-job training programs and collaborative efforts with journalism schools to broaden educational opportunities for students from deprived backgrounds. They have sent their scouts out to look for black talent from every possible source, from the amateur contest on up.

But like the attempts of all our institutions to create job opportunities and training programs for minority people, the effort is piecemeal. The media are not unique and perhaps there is no special warrant for asking them to take the lead where other institutions have also failed. Yet because of their visibility and impact, they can become a bellwether, signaling what systematic institution-wide effort might accomplish.

It is going to take substantial funds and effort to design a program that will bring significantly greater numbers of minority group members into media employment. For problems of recruitment and specialized training are formidable. But such an effort seems to offer the best and perhaps only prospect for supplanting the tokenism that still characterizes most of the media's employment practices.

FIVE

THE SCHOOLS AND PREJUDICE: FINDINGS[1]

M. BREWSTER SMITH

How shall we approach the large and intricate topic of the schools and prejudice? The family, the church, and the school —these are the major institutions for the socialization of the young, for inducting them into their roles as participants in the social order. In our secular times of accelerating social change, both family and church have suffered attrition in their traditional functions. Families, moreover, are hardly more accessible to concerted influence than the individual citizens of whom they are composed. The churches, on their part, no longer reach all children, and they speak to their participants with less assurance and authority than in times past. The school has thus become the pre-eminent institution through which the perspectives and social orientations of new generations are accessible to influence. We probably ought to reject the romantic conception of school as an Archimedean fulcrum through which leverage can be brought to bear on

[1] The research drawn upon here was supported by grants from the Anti-Defamation League of B'nai B'rith to the Survey Research Center, University of California, Berkeley, for a program of research on prejudice under the general direction of Professor Charles Glock. I am indebted to Mr. Oscar Cohen of the Anti-Defamation League for his encouragement and patience and to my colleague in the research, Dr. Jane Allyn Hardyck, to whom major credit should go for the execution of the study.

society to reform or reconstitute it; the American school system with its traditions of local autonomy is too deeply and complexly embedded in society for that. Nevertheless we must still turn to the school if we wish to rear children who are better fitted for participation in a pluralistic democracy. We must still look to it if we want to understand and to change the processes that keep producing new generations of American citizens who are only partly equipped for democratic participation—and in some ways are badly disqualified for it.

How, then, are we to approach this central and difficult topic? A number of options are open to us.

The ghetto school with its mare's nest of acute and chronic problems has recently attracted belated public attention. As described by Kenneth Clark,[2] Herbert Kohl,[3] Jonathan Kozol,[4] and James Herndon,[5] the school in the core city ghetto is all too likely to represent an educational system that is *itself* prejudiced against the slum child—especially the Negro slum child. It prejudges the child's life chances, and arranges matters so as to confirm its pessimistic prophecies. It disparages the child, and, by undermining the basis on which he could develop self-respect and a sense of efficacy, it cripples his inborn human potentialities for taking advantage of the meager opportunities that remain open to him. It subjects the child to all manner of indignities. The system is manned by teachers and administrators who themselves have more or less prejudiced attitudes. Given their difficult and thankless task and their scant resources for coping with it,

2 Kenneth B. Clark, *Dark Ghetto* (New York: Harper & Row, 1965).

3 Herbert Kohl, *36 Children* (New York: New American Library, 1967).

4 Jonathan Kozol, *Death at an Early Age: The Destruction of the Hearts and Minds of Negro Children in the Boston Public Schools* (Boston: Houghton Mifflin, 1967).

5 James Herndon, *The Way It Spozed to Be* (New York: Simon & Schuster, 1968).

prejudice against their educationally unsuccessful pupils is a last bitter line of self-defense. But discrimination against slum children, prejudgment of the child's fate, is built into the system itself. The individual attitudes of teachers and administrative staffs are only components of the system, not prime causes or, probably, even strategic ones. If we are looking for the glaringly acute problems of prejudice and the schools, matters of national shame that cry out for drastic remedy, we should surely start with the system itself.

Or we might consider how prejudice is built into the materials of the school curriculum to which virtually *all* children are exposed—innocently by the purveyors of prettified textbooks designed to appeal to middle-class selection committees, or not so innocently, when publishers edit their offerings to appeal to a national market that includes the South. Self-conscious attention to this problem has doubtless led the writers of recent school texts to pay more attention to America's ethnic diversity and to Negro history and to black contributions to American life. But this attention is not given very often or very honestly, for it is hard to be honest with children about the embarrassing facts. For the most part, the new textbooks make only feeble gestures in this direction; they color a few of the smiling faces black. The persistently bland middle-class orientation of most school materials subtly purveys prejudice, both to the middle-class child, who is given a censored and misleading picture of the society in which he is later to play a part, and to the slum child, who cannot find his own experience validly represented and must conclude that it is a matter for suppression and shame or that school is something irrelevant, to be endured and resisted, an agency of "their" world, not of his own.

Or we might start with the young child as he enters the school system. This is a child who has already acquired some crude social categories for sorting people into "good guys" and "bad guys," who already has his own notions of group identity, who has absorbed from his parents and from the ever intrusive TV some of the adult culture of prejudice but who is still relatively innocent, open and fluid, inconsistent, ready to be educated. We might follow his career to learn how his school experience works upon his initial beliefs and attitudes. We badly need such a longitudinal perspective on the development of prejudice and of democratic orientations, in which the role of the school could be seen in interplay with that of the family, of peer groups, and of the mass media in the lives of individual children. Nobody has done such a study yet.

Or we might start at the other end, with the adult products of schooling, taking heart in the secular trend toward greater acceptance of minority groups, toward less agreement with anti-Negro and anti-Semitic statements, as reported by the national polls over the last generation as the educational level of the population has steadily risen. We could note with Stouffer[6] that younger and better educated people are more tolerant generally than their less educated elders, and with Stember[7] that higher levels of education go with less prejudice. Surely we need now all the sources of optimism that we can glean, and the secular trend toward decreased prejudice is one of these. But we would only delude ourselves if we were to credit the schools with this trend. The decrease in anti-Semitism accompanied not only the world-wide shock at Nazi horrors but also the disappearance of the ghetto Jew as an American social type and his replacement by second- and third-generation Americans—increasingly inappropriate tar-

[6] See S. A. Stouffer, *Communism, Conformity, and Civil Liberties* (Garden City, New York: Doubleday, 1955).

[7] See C. H. Stember, *Education and Attitude Change* (New York: Institute of Human Relations Press, 1961).

gets for prejudice. The decline in anti-Negro prejudice (we can hardly count on its continuing) has paralleled the emergence of a Negro middle class and the articulation of civil rights goals that have the blessing of the established majority elite, as well as of Negro leadership. The inverse relationship between educational level and prejudice may mean only that the better educated are more sophisticated, more in tune with the spirit of the times, more closely in touch with liberal values. Those who go on to the higher levels of education are initially a select group, whose qualities—including being less prejudiced—cannot be credited with any assurance to the schools.

The study that I will draw upon here, conducted by Jane Hardyck and me, ambitious as it was, tried to come to grips with only a small part of the problem of prejudice and the schools. We decided at the outset to focus on the development of patterns of prejudice among teen-agers in junior and senior high school—an age, it seemed to us, when the attitudes that young people will carry into adulthood become stabilized, and also—in American culture—a period of potential youthful idealism when young people should be particularly responsive to democratic influences.

Study Design

Through the Survey Research Center at Berkeley, we had the facilities and skills available for a survey-style study of intergroup relations and attitudes in adolescence. This style of research, as its practitioners well know, lends itself to subtle analyses of interrelationships but runs the risk of overweighting what people say as compared with the more consequential things that they do. We could hardly expect to catch virulent instances of hostile and discriminatory behavior in our net, which was primarily suited for getting at the beliefs and attitudes that young people are able to report when speaking in confidence. So we set a particularly high priority on securing valid data in one area close to actual behavior where survey methods can go beyond "mere" expressions of belief and feeling: friendship choice. We wanted especially to know the extent to which students' choices of friends cross ethnic and religious lines. We could find this out by the simple expedient of asking students to name their best friends (a straightforward approach that has been dignified by the label of "sociometric method") and then collating these answers with the responses of the students *named* to find the self-identified ethnic and religious membership of each. We could collect the data on friendship before the topic of prejudice and intergroup relations had ever been raised, so as to avoid possible distortion on the part of students who knew the democratic "right answer" and might wish to make a favorable impression. But to map out these friendship patterns required that all the friends named also be included in the study, and that each student's ethnic and religious membership be self-identified independently.

To secure such unambiguous data on friendship choice, we decided to include *all* the students in entire grades of entire school systems in the study, thus deliberately giving up the advantages of scope and representativeness that a national sample would have offered. As it was, the data that we wanted stretched the tolerance of school administrators and school boards. Of necessity we had to invade regions of considerable privacy. Students had to name names; they had to shed their anonymity temporarily so that their own ethnic identity could be entered in the sociometric analysis; they were also asked quite personal questions about themselves, their beliefs and feelings, and their family backgrounds. Considerable school time was required for the undertaking—three class hours spaced a week apart. This was a lot to ask for, and many school administrators thought, understandably, that it was too much.

In our initial attempt, we were thrown out of our own Berkeley school system in the fall of 1962. We ended, fortunately, with the full cooperation of three school systems in the East: one, near metropolitan New York, which we call "Commutertown"; another, also in the urban East but farther from New York, which we call "Oceanville"; and a third Eastern industrial city in the midst of a rural area outside any metropolitan orbit, "Central City." By good fortune rather than by design, all three systems turned out to have about the same proportion of Negro students—14 or 15 per cent. And they varied dramatically in the proportion of Jewish students: 43 per cent in Commutertown, 27 per cent in Oceanville, and less than 1 per cent in Central City.

Of course, the three communities were far from comparable in other respects—we can't claim a neat "experimental design." Commutertown was clearly the most sophisticated, and its Negro students included children of middle-class professionals. Central City had larger numbers of blue-collar industrial workers and few Catholics. In each of the three communities, we studied the entire tenth and twelfth grades in the central high school, and the eighth grades in the elementary schools or junior high schools that fed into it. We collected our data in 1963. We are dealing here with substantial numbers of students—2,300 in Commutertown who identified their own race and religion and were therefore suitable for our analyses, 1,200 in Oceanville, and 1,800 in Central City. But it must be remembered that despite the safeguards provided by variation in community characteristics and by the use of large numbers, our study was not representative of the United States. It did not include the segregated ghetto high schools of major Northern cities, nor did it extend to the South or to rural or small-town America.

Thus, our focus on intact grades in the differing school systems of three very different communities obviously does not allow us to generalize safely about levels of prejudice among teen-age students in the nation at large. Indeed, it makes no sense to add up our results across the three school systems: we kept them separate throughout our analysis. But our strategy has other advantages besides the possibility of yielding valid data on intergroup friendship. The causal processes that engender, support, or modify prejudiced attitudes are embedded in school and community; they may differ from one school system to another. Our approach gives us the chance to detect such differences when they exist, and not wash them out in national averages. Where relationships hold across communities as diverse as Commutertown, Oceanville, and Central City, we can have a good deal of confidence in their general relevance. Where the relationships differ, we have the opportunity to track the differences down to special features of particular situations, and, hopefully, to move through these particulars to a higher level of generalized understanding of the underlying processes.

Main Findings

Here I shall only draw selectively on some of the main findings, using a broad brush, in anticipation of our detailed report. A good starting point is the picture of in-group and intergroup friendship that emerged from our analysis of the sociometric data.

FRIENDSHIP CHOICE

We had asked each student to name his or her five closest friends of the same sex and grade. (Responses of boys and girls were analyzed separately.) For each category of student, defined jointly by race (Negro-White), religion (Catholic-Protestant-Jewish), sex, and grade in school, we first examined the extent to which the students' choices of friends were concentrated within their own racial-religious group. This analysis made use of an index that takes into account the proportions of students of each race and religion who are available as possible friends in each sex, grade, and school. A first fact—hardly surprising as it reflects one of the more dependable constants of social human nature—is that in all three communities, students tend to choose their friends from their own racial-religious group. This is particularly true of Jewish students and even more so of Negroes. Among white Protestant and Catholic boys and girls, this tendency toward in-group choice is by no means extreme. There is some trend from the eighth to the twelfth grade for an increasing proportion of choices to go to the in-group.[8]

The same data can be looked at to answer the further question: Do students belonging to the two "minority" groups, Jewish and Negro, *receive* friendship choices from members of the other ethnic-religious categories in proportion to their representation in each sex and grade? Of course, they do not. The indices of cross-group choice to Jews and to Negroes are overwhelmingly negative, with the exception of white Protestant boys and girls in one of the Oceanville eighth grades and white Protestant girls in one of the Commutertown eighth grades; these name Jewish friends at a level a bit higher than chance.

But the story is clearly different for Jews and for Negroes.

[8] Our data are cross-sectional, not longitudinal (following the same individuals through time), so caution is in order here and elsewhere in drawing inferences about trends. We have considerable confidence in these inferences, however, since differences between eighth, tenth, and twelfth grades generally hold up for smaller special samples from which transfers into the schools and dropouts (as of a year later) are eliminated.

In Commutertown and Oceanville (the two communities in which there are enough Jewish students to make this analysis possible), white Catholic and Protestant high school seniors underchoose Jewish students as friends at a level represented by indices ranging from −.15 to −.87 (where −1.00 represents total exclusion and 0 represents nondiscrimination in friendship); the mode is around −.50. As for choices of Negroes for friends, there are very few in any of our three communities, at any grade level. At the twelfth grade, our indices for the various choosing groups center around −.95. The indices are near the absolute ceiling of underchoice; indeed, there is not enough variability to permit us to explore the factors that are linked to friendship with Negroes, either as causes or as effects.

Thus far, then, we have learned that students in each ethnic-religious group tend to find friends among themselves; Gentile students somewhat underchoose Jews as friends, and white students hardly choose black ones at all. (Incidentally, Negro students name whites as friends substantially more often than they are named by whites—an indication of where the problem lies.) I would not want to ascribe these findings *entirely* to prejudice. Although it has become customary in the social sciences to use "ethnocentrism" as a fancy synonym for prejudice, one can prefer one's own, and preferentially seek one's friends from among them, without derogating the other. In a pluralistic society, which finds value in diversity, we should expect and even welcome some persisting bias toward choice of friends from within one's own ethnic or religious group. But the virtually unpenetrated barrier against even same-sex friendships between Negro and white students clearly reflects prejudice. And at the same time, it is itself a major obstacle to the reduction of prejudice. Desegregation that fails to lower this barrier remains in essential respects a token gesture.

WHO CHOOSES JEWS?

So far, we have been examining the patterns of friendship choice that prevail among broad ethnic-religious categories of students. Our next step is to inquire about the social characteristics that go with naming a friend from a religious or ethnic group other than one's own. But we have already seen that so few of our white students name Negro friends that we cannot pursue the question in regard to intergroup choices of Negroes. So we are left with the alternative question, echoing the old jingle, "Who chooses Jews?"

Our analyses of the social characteristics of non-Jewish white students that go with their naming a Jewish friend suggest that two indices, taken jointly, go far toward accounting for whether a student in Commutertown or Oceanville, where the possibility exists, will indeed have a Jewish friend. The first combines several aspects of family background: whether the student is Protestant or Catholic, whether his father does white-collar or blue-collar work, and whether his father's educational level is relatively high or low. (In each case, the first term mentioned goes with intergroup friendship.) These are student characteristics that the school cannot do anything about; they are aspects of its input. The second index, on the other hand, combines three features of the student's school experience: whether or not his eighth grade school was attended by a substantial proportion of Jewish students, whether or not he participates in extracurricular school activities, and whether or not he is enrolled in the college preparatory program.

Figure 1 shows the degree to which these two indices, taken jointly, can predict whether a "majority" student in Commutertown or Oceanville will name a friend who is Jewish. Up and down in the chart are differences in our index of family background; from left to right is our school index.

Who Chooses Jews ?

Percentage of non-Jewish white students who name at least one Jewish friend:

SCHOOL INDEX

Commutertown

FAMILY BACKGROUND INDEX	Low		Medium Low		Medium High		High	
	N	%	N	%	N	%	N	%
Low	46	15	60	17	24	46	9	*
Medium Low	48	15	66	31	55	51	27	78
Medium High	6	*	23	48	35	63	37	78
High	4	*	12	50	34	76	37	86

Oceanville

	Low		Medium Low		Medium High		High	
	N	%	N	%	N	%	N	%
Low	25	8	22	23	13	54	5	*
Medium Low	37	8	51	31	65	46	31	61
Medium High	3	*	38	26	57	46	22	41
High	5	*	14	29	42	52	25	72

*Too few cases to warrant reporting.

Note that only 8, or 15 per cent, of the students who are low on both indices have a Jewish friend, while 72, or 86 per cent, of those who are high on both indices name at least one.

We began this analysis with the thought that the two indices represent the familiar factors in friendship of similarity and propinquity: Gentile students who are higher on the index of family background are more similar to the Jewish students in their schools, and those who are higher on the school index are thrown into more frequent interaction with Jews—and friendship should therefore thrive. The only trouble with this interpretation is that two closely similar indices that are usable in all three communities[9] correlated not only with friendly *attitudes* toward Jews, but with friendly attitudes toward Negroes as well, where the argument from similarity and propinquity does not hold. The revised school index, based only on participation in activities and in the college prep program, is a particularly strong and consistent predictor of unprejudiced attitudes. It looks as though this index reflects the influence of liberal values and life styles as much as that of opportunity for friendly contact.[10]

Opportunity for friendly contact between groups, reflected unambiguously in the ethnic balance of the student's eighth grade school as a component of our school index, clearly influences the development of friendships and, as we shall see later, of unprejudiced attitudes, in its own right. Its influence accounts for part, but not all, of the difference between Cath-

[9] Since Central City had very few Jewish and relatively few Catholic students, religious preference had to be omitted from the index of family background, and composition of eighth grade school from the school index.

[10] Note in Figure 1 that in both communities the school index is related to friendship with Jews, but the index of family background—which is substantially a matter of social class—shows a clear relationship only in Commutertown. When we turn from actual friendship to data on attitudes, the relationship of social class to prejudice, which was marked in Commutertown, also failed to appear consistently in the other two communities. This is one of the community-specific findings that our study highlights.

olic and Protestant students in friendships with Jews, as can be seen in Figure 2. Catholic students who entered the public high school from parochial school were of course barred from school contacts with Jews during their parochial years; their friendships with Jewish students, if they were to develop at all, began after they entered the public high school where we encountered them. This account of the difference they show from Catholics who had attended public school seems the most plausible one, though specific influences of parochial school teaching or of differential family background cannot be excluded.

Even though the subjects of our study were adolescents, the role of their parents should not be totally ignored. The students reported substantial pressures from their parents against Jewish-Gentile friendships. These pressures, as the students report them, are greater for twelfth graders than for eighth graders, are stronger for girls, and increase most over the grades among students who are dating. Our data suggest that parental pressures in Jewish families may actually restrict the friendships of their children. For Gentile students, the picture is inconclusive: parental pressures may be effective in Oceanville, but seem even to backfire in Commutertown where the school leaders are Jewish.

PREJUDICE AGAINST NEGROES AND JEWS

From patterns of friendship we can now turn to attitudes. We used two principal measures of prejudiced attitudes. One was an index of "social distance," or willingness to accept minority persons in social relationships of varying intimacy; the other was an index of agreement or disagreement with unfavorable beliefs or "stereotypes." We could not safely assume that prejudice when it exists extends to all members of ethnic groups that differ from one's own: perhaps students

Religion, Parochial School, and Friendship Choice

Percentage of non-Jewish white students who name at least one Jewish friend:

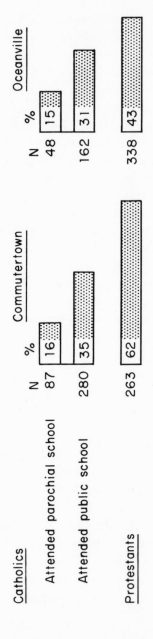

		Commutertown	Oceanville
Catholics	N	%	N	%
Attended parochial school	87	16	48	15
Attended public school	280	35	162	31
Protestants	263	62	338	43

might feel differently about fellow teen-agers from minority groups and minority members of the adult world. With half the students, we therefore inquired about their attitudes toward minority adults; with the other half, about their attitudes toward minority teen-agers.

The measure of social distance presented the students with four hypothetical people in turn (either adults or fellow teenagers of the same sex as themselves): two Jews and two Negroes, whose relative social status was indicated by information about their educational level and job, for the adults, or about their school program (academic or vocational) and average grades, for the teen-agers. About each of these "stimulus persons," the students were asked ten items, representing different degrees of intimacy. Results for a representative item in the more intimate half of the scale—willingness to have "as a close personal friend"—are shown in Figure 3. About three-quarters of the students say they would be willing to have a high status Jew as a close personal friend—perhaps a high figure, but remember that one quarter would not. Note also that while a third to a half of the students say they would similarly accept a high status Negro, we have already seen that very few of the students actually named any Negro among their five best friends.

The measure of prejudiced beliefs was based on the student's degree of agreement or disagreement with twenty items suggested by previous research on anti-Semitic and anti-Negro prejudice. Figure 4 shows comparative results for seven representative items, including one favorable item concerning intelligence. We have adjusted our net here to catch even the mild prejudice of agreeing "a little" to each item.

Our major analyses employed summary scores based on all ten social distance and all twenty belief items. The salient facts for our present purposes are

1. Children come into the eighth grade already furnished with prejudices. They do not change greatly in prejudice, for better or worse, over the high school years.

2. Over the grades, there is a trend toward some decrease in expressed social distance toward Jews (counter to the trend we observed in *actual* intergroup friendships). In regard to Negroes, what changes appear are in the direction of increased social distance. Community differences appear in regard to social distance toward Negroes—most in Central City, least in Commutertown—but not in social distance toward Jews.

3. In regard to acceptance of unfavorable beliefs about Jews, the two communities with appreciable numbers of Jews show an *increase* in stereotyping from grade eight to grade twelve. (Central City, with few Jews, shows some decrease.) The contrast with the trend for social distance is one of the puzzles in our data. In general, the larger the proportion of Jews in the community, the more the stereotyping by the non-Jewish whites.

4. Prejudice is not all of a piece. While in all communities and samples, there are positive relationships between various indices of prejudice—of beliefs, feelings, and preferred social distance—and between prejudice toward Jews and toward Negroes, these relationships are only modest. Prejudice toward minority teen-agers appears to be somewhat less firmly structured than prejudice toward adult members of minority groups (most likely because it depends more on the student's own varied experience with the objects of prejudice and less on cultural transmission), and it enters into a somewhat different pattern of relationships. As for the *content* of prejudice, the profile of anti-Semitism most closely resembles the profile of anti-Negro attitudes in that community (Central City) where there are virtually no Jews; the resemblance is least in heavily Jewish Commutertown. In the absence of Jews, attitudes toward Jews evidently reflect generalized ethnic

A Component of "Social Distance"

Percentage of non-Jewish white students who expressed willingness to have "as a close personal friend".

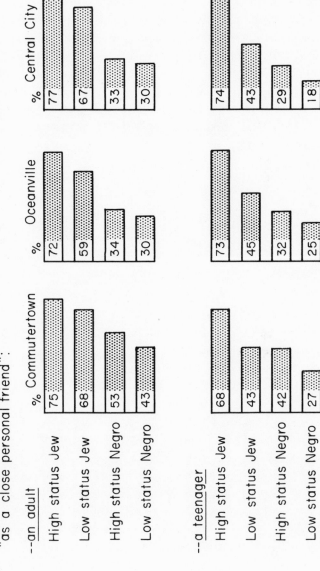

Prejudiced Beliefs

Percentage of non-Jewish white students who agree at least "a little" to the following items:

--about Jewish or Negro adults

	Commutertown (Negro/Jewish)	Oceanville (Negro/Jewish)	Central City (Negro/Jewish)
Dishonest in dealings	52 / 37	46 / 38	58 / 35
Think they are better	44 / 66	37 / 58	64 / 39
More loyal to own group than to U.S.	44 / 41	45 / 40	58 / 43
Intelligent, well-informed	30 / 74	28 / 76	31 / 72
Loose in morals	60 / 44	69 / 31	76 / 29
Push in where not wanted	71 / 33	74 / 38	81 / 27
Don't keep property up	62 / 20	77 / 11	77 / 20

--about Jewish or Negro teenagers

	Commutertown (Negro/Jewish)	Oceanville (Negro/Jewish)	Central City (Negro/Jewish)
Selfish, concerned only for selves and own group	54 / 58	39 / 54	56 / 30
Think they are better	49 / 68	36 / 62	60 / 33
"Butter-up" teachers	21 / 57	15 / 60	31 / 33
Intelligent, well-informed	23 / 72	33 / 80	36 / 71
Loose in morals	69 / 47	65 / 33	69 / 26
Push in where not wanted	52 / 39	41 / 45	67 / 30
Personnally sloppy	58 / 17	64 / 15	61 / 21

Legend: ▨ Negro   ☐ Jewish

prejudice, especially where attitudes toward minority adults are concerned.

5. As we would expect, prejudice toward Negroes is very substantially stronger than prejudice toward Jews, on all measures and in all communities.

6. In the two school systems that have appreciable numbers of Jewish students, Jews are much *less* prejudiced than white Gentiles toward Negroes, and slightly less prejudiced toward white Gentiles than the latter are toward Jews. When we examined the attitudes of Jewish students to members of their own group, we found little indication of so-called "Jewish self-hatred" among these young people.

7. Our data produced no evidence for specifically Negro anti-Semitism. On the whole, the Negro students were if anything somewhat *less* anti-Semitic in their feelings and beliefs than the non-Jewish white students in the same schools. Their slightly greater social distance (in two of the communities) seems an inevitable reaction to the social realities that in fact exclude them from real friendship with virtually all white students, Gentile or Jewish.

VALUE SIMILARITY AND PREJUDICE

We were particularly interested in identifying factors related to prejudice that might furnish leverage for remedial action in the school. One such appeared dramatically in the results of a restudy by Dr. David Stein of the Commutertown eighth graders when they reached the ninth grade.[11] In a complex research design (the sort that earns one a Ph.D.), he got the ninth-graders to indicate their feelings and preferred

11 See D. D. Stein, "The influence of belief systems on interpersonal preference: A validation study of Rokeach's theory of prejudice." *Psychological Monographs*, No. 8 (1966), (Whole No. 616); and for confirming information, D. D. Stein, Jane A. Hardyck, and M. B. Smith, "Race *and* belief: An open and shut case," *Journal of Personality and Social Psychology* I (1965), 281–89.

social distance toward several fictitious students, part of whose purported questionnaires from the previous year were excerpted as a basis for reaction. Background information about the race and social status of the fictitious students was varied systematically, as were also each fictitious student's supposed responses to a set of questions about his personal values —so as to present fictitious response patterns either very much like the student's own (as determined the year before) or contrasting with his own. For white Gentiles, Jews, and Negroes alike, similarity or dissimilarity of personal values turned out to be a far more powerful determinant of liking and social distance than is social status, race, or religious affiliation—a finding very much in line with the theories of prejudice advanced by Milton Rokeach.[12]

But there is a catch. When information is *not* available about similarity of beliefs and values—and in real life this information remains hidden except in intimate relationships —the students' preferences, by default, are much more strongly influenced by the race and religion of the "stimulus person" and, to a lesser extent, by his status. Moreover, when "majority" students are asked to give their feelings about an otherwise unspecified "Negro teen-ager"—embedded in a long list of kinds of people that our main study inquired about—they react to this unspecified teen-ager much as they do to the *particular* Negro teen-ager whom Stein presented as having lower status and values unlike the respondent's own. Prejudice reveals itself in the *assumption* of dissimilarity.

Clearly there are implications here for the kind of educational experience that might penetrate and dislodge prejudiced attitudes. If young people can get to know one another well enough to discover essential similarities where they had

12 See M. Rokeach, *The Open and Closed Mind* (New York, Basic Books, 1960).

previously assumed differences, prejudice can crumble. But they must *encounter* one another for that to happen. Cross-racial encounters at this level of intimacy were rare events indeed in our three school systems.

SCHOOLS, TEACHERS, AND PREJUDICE

So far, we have been talking about the patterns of friendship and prejudice among adolescents in three school systems. We have said nothing about the schools and the teachers. We have almost treated the schools as "catchment areas"— mere geographical locations where eighth, tenth, and twelfth graders can be counted upon to be when you look for them. So far as deliberate teaching or programming for intergroup education is concerned, the metaphor is not far amiss. Not much was going on.

Our data, to be sure, contain hints of things going on among the students themselves that affect their attitudes toward other groups. In Commutertown, for example, where school life is dominated by a mainly Jewish leading crowd, the distinctive relationship that appears there between social class and prejudice seems to be the consequence of a class-linked polarization of informal student leadership that is also polarized along religious lines. White Protestant and Catholic students who belong to the in-group of the Jewish dominated system tend to set their followers a pattern of very favorable attitudes toward Jews. But there is a second, lower-class leading crowd of outsiders, in which white Gentile participants tend to be more anti-Semitic than their followers. It seems likely that their antagonism to the official school leaders as upper-crust Jews has much to do with the relation between social class and prejudice in Commutertown high school.

But what of the teachers? In each of the schools, we asked

teachers of the classes included in the study to fill out a questionnaire that focused on their own experiences with intergroup incidents and with educational approaches to promote better intergroup relations. Not all the teachers cooperated, but most did, presumably including the ones who were most constructively involved with the topic. A majority of them indicated that matters concerning minority groups or intergroup relations should be discussed in a matter of fact way when they come up, in or out of class. The striking finding, however, is how very little they claimed to have actually discussed these matters. Only a third said they had ever discussed Negro history and culture in class, and only a fourth any issue of Negro-white relations. For the corresponding Jewish topics, the proportions were about a fourth and a tenth. Very few claimed to have discussed intergroup topics with individual students outside of class. And we may be sure that these very rough figures are substantially inflated.

I would not claim that talk by teachers and classroom discussions are the only ways, or the best ways, that schools can contribute to the education of their students for democratic living in a pluralistic society. Probably they are not: decisions in regard to classroom and activity grouping, for example, are surely more important. But the picture we gain from the teacher questionnaires is one of passivity and unconcern. The results are depressing to inspect.

In summary, the complete barrier that excludes real friendship between black students and white in all three of our school systems is shocking and cannot be accepted for the future. The big problem for the schools studied was not anti-Semitism but anti-Negro attitudes and behavior. The fact that cross-group friendships were most likely to develop on the part of students who spent the eighth grade in ethnically well-balanced schools is important and encouraging. This is a finding we can do something about. It indicates that desegregation is a minimal condition for the development of good intergroup relations and attitudes. But desegregation per se is not enough. It is also important that similarity of beliefs and values overrides considerations of race and religion—when students know one another well enough to become aware of the similarities that exist. Unless schools take steps to encourage communication and human encounter, students will go their way ignoring members of other groups on the assumption that they are "different."

At bottom, our story is one of the school's missed opportunities—of what did *not* happen educationally to these teenagers, not of what happened. Change in prejudice was minor —but then, nobody was trying very hard to do anything about it.

THE SCHOOLS AND THE FIGHT AGAINST PREJUDICE

CHARLES E. SILBERMAN

This paper will address itself to a broad look at what the schools can and have done to combat prejudice, given the demands imposed by society on the schools. It will also consider the nature of the role the school inescapably plays in this fight—a role I hold to be essentially moral. I have no easy answers, only difficult questions.

The School's Problems in Exerting Leverage

Our schools are creatures of our society. Therefore, the most basic question we can ask of our schools is: Can they make the pursuit of justice and the reduction of prejudice major goals if the society as a whole does not? Our instinctive answer, I think, is: Why, yes, of course. In the United States, reformers have always seen the public schools as a principal instrument, frequently *the* principal instrument, of social reform in the interest of a more humane society. "To an extent characteristic of no other institution save that of the state itself," John Dewey wrote, "the school has the power to modify the social order."[1] But this notion that the school

[1] John Dewey, *Moral Principles in Education* (New York: Philosophical Library, 1959).

is a lever to change society runs counter to another equally pervasive and powerful view that the school is a transmitter of society's existing values. In Dewey's words again, "The school is fundamentally an institution erected by society to do certain specific work—to exercise a certain specific function in maintaining the life and advancing the welfare of society."[2] "Help us to change but help us to remain the same," is the inconsistent charge presented to the public schools.

One cannot discuss the role of the school in contributing to the reduction of prejudice without recognizing this inherently schizophrenic position and the limitations it imposes on action. To talk about ways in which the school "might generally use its leverage to produce a more humane society," therefore, we have to ask: How much leverage do the schools really have, how much freedom to change a society whose values they are also bound to transmit? The answer, I suspect, is that they have a good deal less leverage than most of us outside of the schools generally think they have but a good deal more than most teachers and administrators think they have and than they are currently applying.

Teachers' and administrators' sense of impotence is understandable; people are usually more aware of the limitations on their power than they are of the power itself. This is why executives of large corporations are generally so puzzled by radical attacks on their power. The executive sees himself as hemmed in on all sides by employees, customers, stockholders, competitors, and so on. But more important, as David Riesman has argued,

> The basic vulnerability of the teacher is not, like the administrator, to the pressures from the parents and other veto groups in the community, damaging as these can be to his feeling security and width of maneuver, but rather to the need to be

[2] *Ibid.*

liked by the children, the need to have evident and immediate response.[3]

The weakness of the teachers and the administrators, that is to say, is as much self-imposed as it is imposed from the outside.

At the same time, we need to recognize that we may be asking the schools to do more than they are presently capable of doing—not more than they *should be* capable of doing, however. The schools are not the "balance wheel of the social machinery" that Horace Mann envisaged. They never have been. We have greatly exaggerated and romanticized the role they have played in the last century or so in promoting equality and justice. In point of fact, the schools have always been essentially middle-class institutions. They have never done much of a job of educating children from the lower class, which means they have not done much of a job in promoting wider democracy. Lawrence Cremin writes:

> My own studies have led me to the hypothesis that the common school in its classic form was essentially a Northern and Western phenomenon and that it reached its apotheosis in rural and small-town America west of the Alleghenies. It thrived best where there was already a reasonable homogeneity of race, class, and religion, and where communities were not so large as to permit the development of substantially dissimilar ghettoes. Wherever social or physical distance did become great, as in the South or the large cities, the public school tended to be less "common."[4]

It is not only the "commonness" of the public schools that we have exaggerated; we have also exaggerated and roman-

---

3 David Riesman, *Constraint and Variety in American Education* (New York: Doubleday-Anchor Books, 1958).

4 Lawrence Cremin, *The Genius of American Education* (New York: Vintage Books, 1966).

ticized the role the schools have played in stimulating social and economic mobility for immigrant groups. For a few immigrant groups—the Japanese, the Chinese, the Greeks, the Eastern European Jews—the schools *have* been the critical means of mobility, the critical means of enlarging the democratic base of our society. But these were relatively small numerically and different in ethos from the more numerous immigrant groups—the Irish, the Italians, the Poles. The cultures of the Orientals, the Greeks, and Jews were in many ways compatible with the essentially Protestant ethic of the school, with its emphasis on hard work, achievement, deferred gratification, individualism. The larger immigrant groups— the Irish, the Italians, the Poles—generally made it through politics or business or sometimes through crime. They did not begin to see education, and certainly did not begin to use it, as as means of mobility until *after* they had achieved middle-class status.

Sixty years ago Dewey and the other giants of the early progressive era in education urged the schools to take over the educating and the acculturating functions that had always been performed by family and church—not out of educational imperialism, but because they saw, with considerable prescience, that urbanization and industrialization would greatly weaken and certainly alter the role of these institutions. But the school has not been able to fill that vacuum successfully; we now have documentation, in the Coleman report,[5] the Plowden report,[6] and a number of other studies,[7] that the family, the community, and the adolescent peer-

[5] James S. Coleman, *et al.*, *Equality of Educational Opportunity* (Washington, D.C.: U.S. Government Printing Office, 1966.)

[6] Central Advisory Council on Education, *Children and Their Primary Schools*, 2 vols. (London: Her Majesty's Printing Office, 1967).

[7] E.g., Jesse Berkhead, *et al.*, *Input and Output in Large City High Schools* (Syracuse, N.Y.: Syracuse University Press, 1967).

group can exert influences as great as or greater than that of the school.

The schools have not yet learned how to deal successfully with youngsters from cultures alien to or different from the culture of the school itself. To put it bluntly, we simply do not know how to educate youngsters from the lower socio-economic classes. The pattern of the school is, in effect, to ignore or to destroy the culture that is deviant, to assume that the child must totally adjust himself to the culture of the school. This solution is highly unsatisfactory. A radical alternative is now being proposed by some black separatists and by a number of anti-intellectual intellectuals. They suggest that all the adjustment must be made by the school, that the school accept the culture of the child as given and simply enable the youngster to develop in that cultural direction. This position seems to me to imply a subtle, if unconscious, racism. What it serves to do is to condemn Negro youngsters to remain perpetually *outside* the mainstream of the society.

The plain fact is that there are certain middle-class traits, values, attitudes, or skills, which, while not in any way inherently superior to other culture styles, are nonetheless essential to function in the society that we have. Without highly developed verbal, reading, and analytical-conceptual skills, without pride in workmanship, and planfulness, one is virtually condemned in our society to the life of an unskilled laborer. But we have not learned to reconcile these two equally valid but discrete needs: we do not know how to enable the youngster to move into the dominant middle-class culture without surrendering or destroying for him the separate and significant culture from which he comes.

The failure with economically lower-class children is obvious. But one cannot even be sure that we know very much more about how to educate middle-class children. The schools are a good deal more successful with these youngsters, to be sure, but this may be less because the schools are educating well than simply because the culture of the school is compatible with that of the students.

And so if we ask how much the schools can do to reduce prejudice, the answer, if we are to be honest with ourselves, must be that we do not really know yet. The present is a very sobering period for Americans in a number of ways. Events in Vietnam and Korea have driven home to us the limitations of American military power; the gold crisis has driven home the limitations of the U.S. economic power. And a number of recent research studies (including the study outlined by M. Brewster Smith in the preceding chapter) are driving home to us the apparent limitations of the school's power.

The School's Role as a Moral Role

We have looked briefly at some indications of the limitations of the school's power, historically and presently. Limited or not, the school does play a role in shaping society. What kind of role is it? If we understand the nature of the school's role, we can try more intelligently to modify it in the interest of producing a more humane society.

As we look at what the school does and what it teaches, we are forced, I believe, to acknowledge that the school's function is not simply social or psychological. It is pre-eminently and inescapably moral, what philosophers used to talk about under the rubric of "moral education." I would like to suggest that we revive that term, uncomfortable as it may make us in this age of sophisticated social science. Professor Lawrence Kohlberg of Harvard, who has revived the term, writes:

> For many contemporary educators and social scientists, the term "moral education" has an archaic ring, the ring of the last vestige of the Puritan tradition in the modern school. This

archaic ring, however, does not arise from any intrinsic opposition between the statement of educational aims and methods in moral terms and their statement in psychological terms. Any statement of the social aims and processes of education must be couched in moral terms.[8]

Surely this is true of the specific problems this book is concerned with: the reduction of prejudice and discrimination. The failure of the schools, which Brewster Smith has documented so painstakingly in the previous chapter, is a moral as well as a social and psychological failure. The educational policy decisions that lie at the heart of the school, decisions about what should be taught, in what manner and to what purpose, cannot be made apart from the most fundamental decisions about values and purposes—the values of the society as well as the purposes of education. For what we teach and how we teach reflects, consciously or unconsciously, our concept of the good life, the good man, the good society. There is no educational policy or program that does not have implicit within it some vision of the good life; nor is there any vision of the good life, as Plato taught us, which does not imply some set of educational policies. The failure of the schools is in the last analysis the failure to think seriously and deeply about the aims of education, which is to say about the kind of society and the kind of human beings we want. "It may be a measure of the times," Peter Schrag wrote in a recent article, "Why Our Schools Have Failed,"[9] "that where 40 years ago we produced educational philosophy and ideology, we are now producing statistics." And Robert Dentler, Director of the Center for Urban Education in New York, argues, "If urban educators are failing, they are failing where the newly emergent culture of the urban society itself has

---

[8] Lawrence Kohlberg, "Moral Education in the Schools: A Developmental View," *School Review,* Vol. LXXIV, No. 1 (Spring, 1966).
[9] *Commentary,* Vol. XLV (March, 1968).

failed to specify either ends or means for the educator or his clientele."[10]

Clearly, teachers cannot avoid moral education. "The moral purpose," as Dewey wrote in his unfortunately neglected little classic, *Moral Principles in Education,* "is universal and dominant in all instruction—whatsoever the topic." Children are taught a host of lessons about values, ethics, morality, justice, intergroup relations and attitudes every day of the week, by the way the schools are organized, the way the teachers behave, the standards they set. Even a seemingly innocent remark can be revealing. For instance, the chairman of a New York City high school social studies department was heard to protest after a recent human relations workshop, "Teach human relations? I don't even have time to teach the War of 1812." Little did this teacher realize that he was talking human relations—the worst sort—at that very moment.

These implicit lessons we teach our children are powerful— far more powerful than the verbalizations they often controvert. Children are taught that authority is not to be questioned. Thus, a boy in our local high school was barred from the National Honor Society chapter because he had asked a question critical of the board of education at a public meeting. He asked it in very quiet, respectful tones but implied a criticism of the high school. This, he was told, showed disloyalty to the school and disloyalty to the school showed bad character.

Children are also taught in our schools that people are readily labeled and that the label, no matter how unjust, is hard to remove. In my own community of Mt. Vernon, New York, for example, I witnessed the following incident. It was the first day of school in this suburb haunted by racial tension and token integration and the youngsters of one of the

10 Quoted in *ibid.*

so-called elite elementary schools were filing in. Included among the predominantly white school population was a small minority of Negro children who had been bussed in under a rather feeble open enrollment plan. A handsome young black adolescent entered the building, his white shirt freshly laundered and starched, his pants sharply creased, his face well scrubbed and his hair well brushed. He had the eagerness with which many children begin a fresh year, hoping that they can "wipe the slate clean" if the previous year had been difficult. Before he had managed to maneuver the fifteen feet from the front door to the assembly hall, the principal of the school slapped him on the back with what appeared more strength than playfulness, and boomed out, "Well, Jerry, are you going to behave yourself this year?" With those ten words he managed to dash the hopes of a young boy who wanted to begin the new year with a fresh start. The boy had been tagged and labeled; no matter what he did he was already categorized as a "bad boy."

Children are taught also that docility is to be preferred to dissent, that authority need not be tempered by respect for the people over whom it is exercised. They are taught that what counts is not what you do but whether or not you get caught. They are taught that the object of learning is to get good grades (or to avoid bad grades), and so on. The question, in short, is not whether moral education should be included, but whether it should be done consciously or unconsciously, well or badly.

The ultimate question is how to do it well. I think Dewey had something to say to us on that score, too. He drew a useful distinction between "moral ideas" and "ideas about morality." Moral ideas he defined as "ideas of any sort whatsoever which take effect in conduct and improve it, make it better than it otherwise would be." Ideas about morality are something else again. For, as he wrote, "there is nothing in the nature of ideas about morality, of information about honesty or purity or kindness which automatically transmutes such ideas into good character or good conduct." Most of what the schools do to reduce prejudice and improve intergroup relations, I suspect, represents ideas about morality rather than moral ideas.

This is not to say that teaching about morality, or about justice, equality, prejudice, Negro history, white racism is useless. Quite the contrary. We need a lot more "ideas about morality" in the curriculum and a lot more information that will enable black and white students to understand their history and therefore themselves and their relations. The ignorance that young Negro students have about their history, for example, is dismaying. My son discovered that a Negro friend of his, about to graduate from high school, had never heard of Frederick Douglass, Harriet Tubman, Phyllis Wheatley, William DuBois, James Weldon Johnson, Paul Dunbar, or Marcus Garvey. He thought that George Washington Carver had "something to do with peanuts" and "Booker T. Washington was the guy you're not supposed to like anymore."

To strip a human being of his past this way is outrageously cruel. This is not what the school has done, this is what white society as a whole has done; but having done it, we have a responsibility to contribute to the restoration of the past. To insert a Negro History Week into an all-white curriculum as if it were equivalent to National Pickle Week is patronizing and evasive. Both black and white children need to know that black people did more than pick cotton in the past and scrub floors once a week in the present.

Moral Education: What We Say vs. What We Do

In the last analysis, however, *what* we teach will be less important for the purpose at hand than how we teach, what we do speaks louder than what we say. "It may be laid down as fundamental," Dewey writes, "that the influence of direct moral instruction, even at its very best, is comparatively small in amount and slight in influence, when the whole field of moral growth through education is taken into account." It is this larger area of indirect and vital moral education, the development of character through all the agencies, instrumentalities, and materials of school life that we need to talk about.

If, for example, we fail to treat each child with dignity, if we turn the classroom into a military compound, if we regard total silence except when called upon, and long, straight lines as the criteria by which a teacher's performance are measured —if we do these things, then nothing in the curriculum is going to matter very much when it comes to the question of democracy. If we keep our school segregated by race and class, nothing we say or teach will matter very much when it comes to Negro-white relations. What we do will speak so loud that the children will be unable to hear what we say. Unless the classroom and the schoolhouse become democratic institutions (and I use the word "become" because certainly they are not at this point), we shall not contribute greatly to enhancing a democratic society.

If this sounds harsh, it is because I have been spending some of my time of late inside the schools. It is a sobering and depressing experience. The public school, I can report, is the kind of institution you cannot really hate until you know it well. The anti-intellectualism of the public schools is well known and well documented. One small, personal example of how soon the process works: My youngest child, a third grader, was dissuaded by his teacher from reading E. B. White and the Dr. Doolittle books and urged to read the Little Golden Books and the like. It seems that book reports, which are due weekly, are supposed to be written on

4 x 6 filing cards, and the reports on the books as long as he was reading couldn't fit on the cards. Equally important, one report was required each week, and if he were to read lengthy books, he could not meet the schedule; so he shifted from reading literature to reading junk. This insistence in fitting everything to the mold runs very deep.

Another example of the petty literalness of the schools is provided by a friend at Yale who works in the New Haven schools. He tells the story of the teachers, one after another, coming to him almost in tears the week after President Kennedy's assassination, saying, "What shall we do? We can't teach. The children don't want to talk about anything but the assassination." It never occurred to them that the materials of the curriculum might be postponed a few days for the far more relevant issue at hand.

What is not so well understood as this lack of imagination is the grimness, the joylessness, of American public schools. We have not recognized how oppressive and petty are the rules by which they are governed—rules which students, teachers, principals, superintendents, and parents alike— simply accept as given. There is vastly more joy, laughter, and spontaneity, for example, in Japanese elementary and junior high schools, and a far easier, warmer, more relaxed relation between the students and teachers than in our own. They are friendlier places notwithstanding the enormous classes (fifty students), the uniforms, the group recitations and rote drills, the fact that most Japanese school buildings would be considered decrepit in the heart of the ghetto.

I used to think that the criticisms of Edgar Friedenberg[11] and John Holt,[12] while useful and essentially accurate, were badly overstated. Although I disagree strongly with them on

11 Edgar Friedenberg, *Coming of Age in America* (New York: Random House, 1965).
12 John Holt, *How Children Fail* (New York: Pitman, 1964).

some points, I sometimes wonder now whether their criticisms might perhaps even be understated. We decry, for example, the lack of civility among the young, particularly the young demonstrators—but one seeks in vain for civility in the classroom. What one observes instead is the sheer rudeness with which most teachers speak to children as a matter of course. They don't say "please," they don't say "thank you," they simply give orders with no explanation. If we adults do not respect the youngsters, how can we expect them to respect each other?

Avoiding doing the wrong things, however, which is pretty much what I have been talking about, is not enough. Putting dissimilar people together does not in itself reduce prejudice. The assumption that it does, reflects a naïveté that we need to outgrow—the notion that people are all alike and the unstated belief that if they are not, they should be. On one level, to be sure, people are all alike: "Scratch me deep enough and I bleed." But on another level they are different, and the differences reflect the groups (ethnic, religious, racial, class) to which they belong. We have been badly hampered, I fear, by our own mythology of individualism, which has blinded us to the realities of group differences. The way to reduce prejudice, improve group relations, make the society more humane, is to recognize these differences, not to pretend that they do not exist or that they do not matter. They do exist and they do matter. Racial or religious or ethnic suicide should not be the price of acceptance by anyone else.

We have to learn how to teach our children and ourselves to recognize the similarities beneath the differences; to see that Negroes or Jews or Protestants or Catholics, are in crucial respects very much like us. But it may be more important, although certainly more difficult, to teach them and ourselves to respect others in spite of, or because of, these differences.

It won't be easy; the persistence of racial and tribal and

national animosities everywhere in the world, the outbreaks of racial prejudice among peoples like the British, who prided themselves on their freedom from prejudice bespeak a fear of difference that seems to run very deep in the human being. But the United States, for all its faults, for all the prejudice and discrimination, for all the racism that remains, has gone farther toward creating a truly pluralistic society than any other nation that has ever existed. Having come so far, we surely can go further.

Let me close, then, with a favorite passage from the Ethics of the Fathers. Having written about moral education, I may be forgiven at least one idea about morality. "The hour is late, the time is short, and the Master is urgent. It is not incumbent upon us to complete the task, but neither are we free to desist from doing all that we possibly can."

SEVEN

PREJUDICE IN THE MARKETPLACE

HOWARD J. SAMUELS

Of all the problems crying out for solution in our society today, none is more critical than the plague of prejudice that corrodes American life.[1] Business and organized labor must acknowledge their share in perpetuating these inequities. And it is a large share, indeed. For though all our social institutions have done their bit to perpetuate inferior status, the pocketbook is where the minority American has felt his disadvantage most keenly. Year by year, as the affluence of white America proclaims itself over the television channels, the black American's entrapment in poverty has become more apparent to him—both the cause and the emblem of his second-class citizenship.

The hippies have been teaching us that money cannot buy love. But money can buy decent houses, and education, and even respect—things that are essential if a man is to move up into productive and equal citizenship. Economic equality is the first step—the step that enables him to dress as well as others, to live in as good a house in as pleasant a neighbor-

---

[1] Because the nation is presently engulfed in confronting the consequences of racial prejudice, I have opted to concentrate my observations in this paper on this form of prejudice, especially white prejudice toward blacks. I would ask the reader nevertheless to recognize that what is being said could well apply to other forms of prejudice, all of which are destructive of our nation's best capabilities.

hood, to send his children to as good a school. It is the step that gives him his stake in society and makes him want to preserve and improve that society. This paper will examine where business and industry stand, what they are doing and— more importantly—what they are not doing, what they can and must do to ensure equality of opportunity.

The Report of the National Advisory Commission on Civil Disorders rightly assigned top priority to jobs and rightly attributed the current economic plight of the Negro to the virus of white racism. On both counts, American business and labor must plead guilty. Far from being immune to the disease of racism, they have only just begun to visualize the horizons of meaningful Negro employment. It takes no special awareness of history, for example, to see that a few short years ago it required an extraordinary measure of faith for a young Negro to seek a college education when his only view of the corporate structure was likely to be from the elevator he operated, whatever his educational achievement.

The picture has changed a good deal. There are more corporate doors open, and more are opening every day. Today the educated Negro has prospects before him undreamed of just a decade ago. In the early 1960's, in fact, his chances at times may have been slightly better than those of his white counterpart. Yet the over-all statistics are grim. The Kerner Commission found that "pervasive unemployment and underemployment are the most persistent and serious grievances in minority areas." The facts speak more eloquently than any rhetoric.

Negro median family income is only 58 per cent of white families. And 20 per cent of all Negroes are making "no significant economic gains" despite rising prosperity. The report goes on to detail with unassailable evidence the realities of prejudice in business and industry. The over-all gap between white and nonwhite income remains virtually unchanged in fifteen years, as does the black unemployment rate, which remains consistently more than double the white rate, and in teen-age unemployment, the gap has actually widened.

The report found underemployment even more of a culprit than unemployment. Negroes now hold 63.5 per cent of the jobs in household and other menial services, but they represent only 6 per cent of the professional or technical work force, 3 per cent of business managers or the sales force.

Perhaps the most ominous and yet, paradoxically, most hopeful data are summed up in the Kerner Commission's "profile" of last summer's typical rioter. He was fifteen to twenty-four years of age, somewhat more educated than his nonrioting neighbor, having had at least some high school training before dropping out. He was employed, usually part-time and with frequent interruptions, but almost always in menial, low-status jobs. "He feels strongly," the report indicates, "that he deserves a better job and that he is barred from achieving it not because of lack of training, ability or ambition, but because of *discrimination by employers.*"

This finding is ominous because if these young people are not plucked from the streets and moved into the mainstream now, they will spawn still another generation of ghetto children to be nurtured on the bitter fruit of their parents' justified hostility. This is the case not only for the Negro but for other minorities as well—the Puerto Rican, the Mexican-American, the American Indian.

Yet the profile is also promising. Rebellion is born of hope, however cynically it may be clothed, of a belief in change. In this sense, rebellion is healthier than apathy or despair. Given that spark, and youth, these rioters' lives are changeable. Their expectations are already a step beyond those of the previous generation. But we have to will it—and "we" in this context means the industrial community, assisted by government.

Failure to raise the status of black Americans and other minorities can by no means be blamed entirely on industry. Our educational and social structure has operated to discourage and frustrate their drive for self-betterment. But industry has the opportunity now to make a breakthrough more readily than other sectors. For if business bears a significant part of the responsibility for the *status quo,* at the same time, corporate America stands readier than many other sectors of our society to take on its fair share of the burden of change. The reason is simple: the genius of American business has always been its capacity to perceive its long-term self-interest and invest substantially in the development of that interest, to change with changing times, to retool when necessary, to conserve by innovating rapidly and effectively. This realization has already prompted many changes. Aside from the moral imperative, there is the brute fact that industry cannot operate efficiently in a conflict-torn society.

Industry's Achievements and Shortcomings in Prejudice Reduction

Under the compulsion of law in some instances, under pressure from an increasingly militant black community in others, and out of a growing awareness that discrimination undercuts the dollar, business is in a sense retooling to hire Negroes and other minorities not by the ones or twos, or even by the hundreds, but by the thousands. And it is using the considerable government help at its disposal to do so. Faced with the economic imperative, business is shaping up —slowly, but surely.

There are many examples of widespread activity to reach and train the hard-core unemployed and underemployed. *The Negro and the City*[2] has painted the picture in reason-

---

[2] Adapted from a special issue of *Fortune* on "Business and the Urban Crisis" (New York: Time-Life Books, 1968).

ably accurate if somewhat glowing terms. Hundreds of the biggest U.S. corporations have banded together in a National Alliance of Businessmen in a drive to find, employ, and train 30,000 hardcore unemployed by June, 1968; 100,000 by June, 1969; and 500,000 by the summer of 1971. This is not just a summer drive to get young people off the streets, nor is it a WPA project to get them on a payroll; it represents the training and retaining in real jobs of 500,000 hard-core unemployed, taken permanently off the relief rolls and adapted to useful citizenship. The task will not be easy, but the men who are running this program are moving into it in a systematic and dedicated way.

Businesses are finding new ways to reclaim human resources, often with federal government support. Currently the government is making $350 million available to offset the extra costs of hiring, motivating, and training the hard-core unemployed and pulling them over the first hurdles into what one hopes will be long-term employment. More than 1,600 corporations have contracted to provide training under the Manpower Training and Development Act, which reached 140,000 people in fiscal 1967.

Recently, a number of large corporations located in ghetto areas have decided to train neighborhood manpower at considerable expense rather than follow the white exodus to suburbia (at even greater expense). Despite some cynicism about why business is suddenly showing a spurt of interest, the fact remains that when self-interest is congruent with reduction of inequities, gains are likely to be more rapid and more persistent.

Other industry efforts to reclaim the hard-core unemployed have come in response to government prodding but also often spontaneously. An Aerojet-General subsidiary, responding to government pleas to make work for Watts residents after the 1965 riots, opened a tent-manufacturing plant. Hiring virtually all comers, Aerojet found that, although they had no sew-ing skills and no work experience, these employees, when motivated, learned fast—especially with sympathetic instruc-tion and a piecework incentive system. The company reached the break-even point ahead of schedule, and, two years after the plant's inception, it had a $2,500,000 backlog of orders.

More and more companies have found that, rather than educate so-called unemployables beforehand, they can hire first and then provide whatever training or education is re-quired for the employee to do the job and gain a sense of accomplishment.

The picture is not all rosy; most of the hard core have not been reached, and training efforts are not uniformly success-ful. But the effort is growing, and the stakes are great. The list of companies now trying to train hard-core unemployed includes Avco (with a multimillion-dollar project in Boston's Roxbury section), Goodyear, General Dynamics, Northrup —and the list grows daily. Employing even 350,000 of the hard-core unemployed would increase the national output by more than $1 billion a year and would subtract millions of dollars from welfare costs.

The fight for equality in industry goes beyond the hiring of the hard-core unemployed to require changes in hiring requirements, involvement of industry in civil rights action groups, and direct participation in urban improvement. Hopeful signs can be cited in all these areas. Thus, a recent *Wall Street Journal* survey of fifty major corporations found them playing "a significantly larger role" in the civil rights areas than they had assumed five or even two years ago. The National Alliance of Businessmen and the Urban Coalition (a group composed of businessmen as well as civil rights, re-ligious, and urban affairs leaders) are growing in member-ship, momentum, and money. Top officials of the "big fifty" companies in almost every case have civil rights or urban development affiliations.

Hiring standards have been loosened. The proportion of black workers in most of the big companies has grown considerably over the last five years—their numbers have increased anywhere from three- to tenfold in firms such as RCA, the Bell System, IBM. Some companies, including RCA, and Southern Pacific Railroad are ignoring minor criminal records; other companies have scrapped the requirement of a high school diploma for many jobs.

Even more striking is the growing commitment of industry to civil rights programs in the community. Thus the country's staid life-insurance industry has invested more than $1 billion to improve real estate in the inner-city slums, where until now mortgage money has been unavailable. Some of this money will go through federal channels as insured mortgages to help in housing construction. Other money will be siphoned into high-risk uninsured mortgages—commercial, industrial, and also residential.

In New York City, Chase Manhattan Bank representatives have made visits to 400 Negro-owned businesses in Harlem in search of loan prospects. In San Francisco, Safeway Stores has helped the Negroes of Hunters Point revive a failing cooperative supermarket that in fact competes with a Safeway outlet ten blocks away.

Major corporations such as U.S. Steel and Jones and Laughlin Steel have joined with city-planning offices to make proposals for urban redevelopment. Big companies have also discovered that they can contribute to education, and in this way fight the easier battle of preparing young people from the slums before they reach the job market rather than trying to reclaim them later as dropouts. At Consolidated Edison, New York high school students who have been classified as potential dropouts are hired part-time so long as they stay in school with passing grades. Ohio Bell Telephone offers high school seniors a ten-week Saturday course in basic electricity, for pay, with the promise of jobs for the qualified after graduation. At Ford Motor Company, top management works with the National Alliance of Businessmen and the Urban Coalition; some are on loan to the biracial New Detroit Committee; the company also is helping a small Negro cosmetics firm stay solvent and releasing some of its executives to study the high school system of Detroit.

Business leaders have become more enlightened, and the schools of business that train them—Harvard, Wharton, MIT, and so on—report great ferment with rapidly increasing focus on urban problems and racial crises.

But despite current and proposed changes, despite investment in recruiting and on-the-job training, despite its growing community involvement, industry is still falling far short of both its obligations and its potentialities. Business has not seized its opportunities for leadership as aggressively as it should.

The Equal Employment Opportunity Commission conducted hearings last year into the pattern of discrimination in white-collar employment in 100 major companies in New York City that because of their size and resources should be leading the way. The results are disappointing. "The 100 major companies," the commission found, "clearly fail to match their *economic* leadership with leadership in equal employment opportunity." They even lag significantly behind the New York City average in hiring and promotion of Negroes and Puerto Ricans. "By almost any measure," the commission said, "we find that those who should be the leaders in this crucial area of local and national concern are, in fact, the laggards."

Even those companies that are members of Plans for Progress—companies that have voluntarily initiated programs to end discrimination in their shops and offices—have not been doing all they should. Records of the forty-six companies in this group show that less than 1 per cent of their executive and managerial jobs are held by Negroes.

Furthermore, in almost no instance does the racial composition of an organization approach the racial mix of the community in which it exists. Negro leaders are quick to point out the meaninglessness of some of the statistics—if a company has employed only one Negro and adds one more, the 100 per cent increase this represents is a practical absurdity.

In point of fact, minority employment in nineteen major industrial areas varies widely: the medical services rank highest, with 16.4 per cent Negro employment, followed by the primary metals (12.3 per cent) and food industries (11.1 per cent). At the bottom of the ladder of Negro hiring are the communications field—radio, TV, newspapers, advertising (4.3 per cent)—and finance, insurance, and real estate (3.7 per cent), along with the utilities (also 3.7 per cent).

Numbers do not tell the whole story. The black American tends to be hired at menial or low-level jobs and to stay there, so that large increases in mere numbers are not necessarily encouraging. And some black leaders contend that even the companies that are trying are not effectively reaching the true hard-core unemployed but are simply skimming the top of the minority labor market, leaving untouched the hopeless and alienated ghetto youth. The effort to reach the really hard-core unemployed is, of course, expensive and frustrating. But ours is not an age of easy problems.[3]

3 Although this paper is concerned primarily with the role of business and industry, it is clear that the Negro will not get a fair break in the marketplace until the labor movement, too, searches its conscience and amends its practices. Labor unions have traditionally been progressive agents of change. One need look only at the history of the United Auto Workers, the Steel Workers, the National Maritime Union, among scores of others, to discover decades of dedication to the fight for equal human rights.

But labor's other acts must also be taken into account; of 18 million union

Discrimination vs. Prejudice

Although industry has made a formal commitment, and although it has or can get the necessary money and technical resources, it is still held back by the same kind of prejudice that pervades other institutions. Business has shown concern with *industrial* relations between employer and employee, between supervisor and staff, but it has shown almost no interest through the years in human relations. Until recently management has had little concern for the attitudes of supervisory personnel, attitudes that may influence employment on ethnic or religious grounds.

Taking the bread-and-butter steps to improve conditions and complying with laws, while essential, are not enough. Changes in attitudes are as urgent as changes in overt behavior, for they lay the groundwork for any deep and lasting attempt to expunge prejudice.

That prejudicial attitudes permeate the world of industry and labor, we know from many instances. The breadth and depth of this prejudice we have not tapped, because until re-

---

members in the United States, about 2 million are blacks. They have been left out of the most powerful unions—especially in transportation and the skilled trades. Most of them are concentrated in the semiskilled, unskilled, or service unions. This is partly because of the kinds of jobs Negroes hold, but is also partly the result of a campaign of exclusion. Prime offenders are the building trades, which have not opened their ranks to qualified Negroes and have excluded them from apprenticeships.

Clauses that favor whites in promotions and layoffs are characteristic of large industries such as steel, paper, and tobacco. Other offenses include segregated locals (there are more than 150 all-Negro locals in the AFL-CIO) and the kind of polite tokenism by which a union fulfills the letter—but not the spirit—of a federal law by hiring a small number of blacks. The AFL-CIO requires only voluntary compliance with antidiscrimination provisions and has never yet expelled a union proved guilty of racial discrimination.

Moderate black leaders have suggested as minimum goals the elimination of the union hiring hall, expulsion from the AFL-CIO of unions proved guilty of discrimination, and Labor Department and state agency help in guaranteeing open access into the apprenticeship programs to train much-needed skilled labor.   ·

cently, bigotry—by gentlemen's agreement—was regarded as none of the business of business. In the business world, with its traditional skepticism about social science research and attitudinal surveys directed at its own practices, prejudice is almost impossible to isolate, let alone measure. As a result we have often inferred prejudice from the incidence of discrimination.

When a promising young management type is interviewed at lunch and told, "You look like us, and we can get you into the Detroit Athletic Club," that's prejudice.

When the personnel director of a firm holding a government contract, says of Negro workers, "We have something they can do, simple and repetitive," that's prejudice.

When a group of blacks score spectacularly well in examinations for acceptance for apprentice training in a skilled trade, and some labor officials claim they must have cheated, that's prejudice.

When two-thirds of the private employment agencies queried in New York City—and 87 per cent in key cities across the country—accept an order for a "white Gentile secretary" and comment, "They're always the most capable," or, "We don't place colored," that's not only prejudice, it is also out-and-out unlawfulness.

These instances could be multiplied thousands, if not hundreds of thousands, of times—and they reflect attitudes ingrained in American society for centuries. Somewhere out there, obscured by good intentions and stated devotion to the principle of equal opportunity, lie old but operative convictions that black Americans are inherently inferior, shiftless, lazy, unemployable, and unpromotable; that Jews do not executives make (nor fellow club members); that people less fluent in English than in Spanish are therefore less worthy; that the only good plumber is a white plumber. This is what the Kerner report has tried to tell us.

I am not suggesting that we have failed substantially to reduce bigotry in this country or to lessen its translation into discrimination. I am suggesting that what remains is deeply rooted, often disguised and hence much harder to weed out. Indeed, because *some* progress has been made, we have overestimated the actual reduction of vicious and pernicious stereotypes, and we have underestimated the role these unchanged attitudes continue to play in perpetuating discrimination.

As the hard-core unemployed begin their difficult climb, they collide, therefore, with the hard-core remnant of prejudice. Worse, they face it disguised under a veneer of politeness, even fellowship. For the racism which persists in our society, particularly in the world of business, has gone underground. Those who are infected with it—good "normal" Americans—are often blind to it within themselves. They are like the "light-gray" anti-Semites described in the landmark "Patterns of American Prejudice Series.[4] The "light-gray" anti-Semite is capable of maintaining relationships with Jews in every arena—from the business world to the educational establishment to the living room. Nevertheless, he holds stereotyped notions about Jews that really do not seem offensive to him and are not recognized by him as anti-Semitic.

This kind of prejudice is often guarded or fobbed off onto others, as "we ourselves think it would be great, but some of our best customers might feel funny about a Jewish vice-president." "We ourselves have no objections to Negro salesmen but others don't see it this way."

It is this insidious kind of prejudice that is experienced by minority group members more and more often. Indeed, the disillusionment of the ghetto stems in part from the duplicity

[4] R. Stark and S. Steinberg, "It *Did* Happen Here—An Investigation of Political Anti-Semitism: Wayne, New Jersey" (Anti-Defamation League of B'nai B'rith, 1967).

of the Northern brand of prejudice: promise without performance; sanctimonious lip service to liberalism; equality in law and servitude in fact; good intentions held by good people who don't begin to comprehend the dimensions of the problem and who are quite blind to the prejudice which subtly militates against comprehension.

Whenever a Harlem job applicant is promised equal opportunity yet is given a test wholly alien to his nonwhite frame of reference, wholly neglectful of the differences between ghetto and nonghetto education, and often wholly irrelevant to the job being filled—a subtle prejudice is operating.

The Negro applicant will identify the racism inherent in the test even if the interviewer does not. The result is a widening of the "credibility gap." Closing that gap—the deep conviction on the part of the Negro American that he is unwanted by American business—is a large part of the enormous task now confronting the business community. Whitney Young has said that the gap will be closed only when "the business community consciously and deliberately *in*cludes, as it has consciously and deliberately *ex*cluded." But will prejudice prevail in the marketplace? None of us can be certain it will not unless we move on both fronts simultaneously— the front of practice and the front of feelings, knowing that each reinforces the other.

Some Ways to Begin

Suppose a company really wants to do its part in eliminating both discrimination and the subtler patterns of prejudice. How can it go about this task pragmatically? Experience has shown that the following steps represent a good beginning:

1. *Earnest commitment at the top.* The business leader must be involved in this problem not just in his own business but in his school and church and neighborhood. It is from

him that the staff will pick up cues that will reinforce or weaken the company's program. If the chairman of the board issues a memo to employees stating the company's policy against prejudice and then goes off to play squash at his comfortably segregated club, the commitment is tarnished.

2. *Untiring efforts to propagate that commitment through the ranks.* The commitment must be more than the "take a Negro to lunch" variety, and it must be communicated through the ranks. One organization has taken unequivocal action against members guilty of discrimination: the president of the Association of Personnel Agencies of New York recommended that member agencies fire on the spot anyone found guilty of accepting a discriminatory order. Such discrimination runs counter to the state law in New York, counter to federal law everywhere, and jeopardizes the entire agency.

The best of policies can be sabotaged somewhere down the line. Every middle manager and every foreman must know that his personal interest requires him to participate in the company's drive to eliminate prejudice—that, in fact, prejudice on his part will count against him. Business' alleged need for conformity can be utilized productively in the fight against prejudice by making it clear that the prejudiced employee is out of step.

One fundamental approach that has been very successful is the presentation of workshops for foremen and superintendents to teach them how to work with and train the hardcore unemployed—including the recognition of their own patterns of prejudice. Organizations like the Urban League have worked with industry to set up such workshops.

3. *Examination of recruiting procedures.* Is recruiting being done where minority workers are? The auto companies have found they had to set up a center in the ghettos to re-

cruit successfully among men who did not believe there was any point in going to the plant gate.

A common excuse for not employing blacks and other minority group members is that there are not enough qualified representatives of these groups around. It is true, of course, that minority groups have been deprived so long that they do not readily offer the same pool of talent available elsewhere. It may take extra effort to find them, as well as extra training once they are found. But the fact is that some companies have much better records than others.

In New York, for instance, one top law firm has eleven Negro clerks—yet four others could find none who were qualified. Two of the leading banks have thirty-one black managers—yet four others could find none qualified. A company that throws its talents and resources into finding and placing qualified Negroes or Puerto Ricans or Mexicans or American Indians can apparently find them.

One barrier to locating these people may be the recruiters themselves. If they are stereotype-ridden, they may need an ongoing workshop in intergroup relations. Many human rights organizations would be glad to offer such programs.

4. *Reviewing standards for hiring and promotion.* Are these standards realistic, or are they restricted by the "credentials barrier"? For many jobs education is not the most important criterion, nor is a clean police record essential. For some jobs, the tests administered are neither an accurate nor a fair measure of the applicant's ability to perform. When tests devised for the white middle-class are applied to the ghetto, prejudice is at work.

5. *Establishment of a "systems analysis program" to see that nondiscrimination policies are enforced and that top management gets regular reports.* It is easy for top management to lose track of what is really going on along the line and in the ranks. But business knows how to monitor its opera-

tions when it wants to. It does this every day with other aspects of company policy, like safety. In a well-run company the top brass will get regular reports of safety performance in each division. It will be measured in specific and qualitative terms—numbers of accidents compared with last year, seriousness of accidents, steps taken to prevent further accidents. Managers are rewarded for good performance.

The same kind of systems analysis can be applied to elimination of prejudice. The job is too important to be left to the personnel office, which may too easily play the old numbers game—numbers of Negroes hired this year without an analysis of what jobs they were hired for or of how many left the company out of discouragement about their future prospects.

These five steps can be the key to effective progress in the daily working lives of disadvantaged people. But a wider commitment is also necessary.

6. *The extension of the fight against prejudice—going beyond the plant and out into the community.* One way to do this is by helping minority groups establish and run their own businesses. This is part of the American dream, and the cry from the ghetto means that its citizens too want "a piece of the action." Today less than 1 per cent of the nearly 5 million business enterprises in the United States are owned or operated by nonwhites, and this must be changed.

There are many ways the business community can help. A number of companies have participated in development corporations, for instance, which enable budding entrepreneurs to get bank loans and show them how to run a business successfully. Businessmen can lend their talents directly by helping create a new, independent class of businessmen with a real stake in American capitalism. Government is actively aiding this effort, but the vital ingredient of expert guidance must come from the business community. Other ways in which industry can help outside the plant include the investment of time and money in urban rehabilitation, the underwriting of scholarships for minority group members, the support of open housing legislation that permits workers to have decent homes in decent communities.

Basic to all these efforts is the need to learn about the interior workings of the black community—its aims, its fears, its leaders. Businessmen ought to learn something about the leadership of the minority community *before* trouble develops. They should be prepared to work with the leaders identified by the Negroes or other minority groups themselves rather than try to impose their choice of a tractable spokesman who may be resented by the very people he is presumed to represent.

To organized labor, many of the same strictures apply. Both justice and ultimate self-interest require that unions do not restrict their membership and that the workers they represent are not discriminated against in employment on the basis of race. Unions must also pay increasing attention to civil rights questions outside the realm of employment itself. The education departments of a number of trade unions have made notable efforts to educate against prejudice. The leadership of many unions has insisted on nondiscriminatory clauses in contracts and made vigorous attempts to improve social and economic conditions for minority groups. But the record of labor, as we have noted, has also been sullied by prejudice and restrictive tactics.

The World of Work as the Setting for Understanding

We have spelled out a number of practical recommendations. Yet while all these efforts are crucial, they will not solve the whole problem. For as a recent *Business Week* editorial pointed out, "a deeper prejudice, based on color, is itself a cause of the Negro's failure to advance. Racial prejudice must be dealt with on its own; it cannot be removed simply by improving jobs and education." So while attempts are being made to improve the economic situations by laws, and rules, and vigorously supported policies, we must at the same time come to grips with prejudice where it exists—in the hearts of men.

And it is heartening that it is precisely in the work situations that prejudice may most easily lend itself to eradication. Gordon Allport[5] years ago set forth the conclusion, based upon tested research, on prejudice reduction in specific contact situations. As Allport stated and Campbell and Pettigrew[6] restated the findings, prejudice can be reduced in contact situations characterized by four criteria: (1) the groups in contact possess equal status; (2) they seek common goals; (3) they are cooperatively dependent upon each other; and (4) they interact with the positive support of authority. As Campbell and Pettigrew point out, all four conditions are best met in the working place, where fellow employees (equal status) seek better wages and working conditions (common goals) through a division of labor (cooperative dependence) under the guidance of law and policy (the law of the land and the policy of management).

There are fewer "social" complications in the place of employment than in school or church or neighborhood. In the plant or the accounting department or on the sales staff, people have a common set of goals. In this built-in situation for democratic participation, each man on the assembly line is as necessary as the next. He is judged by the job he does and the contribution he makes. There is less need for him

---

[5] Gordon W. Allport, *The Nature of Prejudice* (New York: Doubleday, 1958).

[6] Ernest Campbell, and Thomas Pettigrew, *Christians in Racial Crisis* (Washington, D.C.: Public Affairs Press, 1959).

to "fit in" socially or live on the right street or have the right parents. It is the best place to begin breaking down walls that divide the races and religions.

In our increasingly suburbanized society, where the little boxes on the hillside are filled predominantly with white people with white children going to white schools—no arena offers so fertile a field for equality as does the world of work. Business and labor have a unique opportunity, an historic opportunity, an opportunity that is equal to the urgency.

As James Baldwin, in *The Fire Next Time,* has written, "We have much to learn from each other, if you can overcome the curtain of my color. You can't go back to Ireland, or England, or Poland—and I can't go back to Africa. We'll either live here together or die here together."

TOWARD THE CONTROL OF PREJUDICE AND DISCRIMINATION IN AMERICAN LIFE

Prejudice and discrimination are woven deeply into the fabric of American life. Nothing that the authors of the previous chapters have said comes through more starkly than this. Yet there is promise in their reports that what is need not always be—that American society has the potential for bringing practice more closely in line with principle.

What precisely is this potential, and how is it to be tapped? Because each author was asked to consider a single institution, none of them addresses himself wholly to answering these overarching questions. But each does make some contributions to answers, and this chapter attempts to draw together these themes to suggest an integrated strategy for controlling prejudice and discrimination in America.

To this end, we shall first set forth briefly what would appear to be required ideally if control is to be effected. We believe this plan to be implicit in what the authors, taken together, have said. Our purpose here will be to try to make it explicit. Having done this, we shall then compare the ideal with the authors' descriptions of the existing situation. This comparison will tell us how much of the potential is already being realized and where the major discrepancies lie. In the closing part of the chapter, we shall consider what might be done concretely to reduce these discrepancies.

The Ideal

Prejudice and, in turn, discriminatory behavior are usually learned early in life. Once learned, they persist because they are never effectively challenged. Their control requires that they not be taught in the first place and also that they not be left unchallenged when they are. There is no agency in the society capable of performing both functions or even one of them entirely on its own. If the job can be done at all, the authors implicitly tell us, it can be done only by a number of social institutions working together.

Preventing the learning of prejudice by children is a different problem from curing the prejudice already learned by adults, and each can be expected to involve different institutions as control agents. Let us look first at the initial learning of prejudice by children. In a utopian society it would be expected that children would never learn prejudice, because no agency of socialization would teach it to them. In real societies this is not assured, and, directly or indirectly, all agencies having a socializing influence may contribute to teaching prejudice. Part of the key to controlling prejudice, then, lies in preventing this kind of deliberate or inadvertent instruction.

Most of this instruction comes earliest and most intensively from the principal agency of socialization—the family. Unfortunately there is not much that society can do to control this source of prejudice. Some effort, of course, might be expended to reduce parental prejudice; we will consider this kind of effort presently. But by and large it is highly unlikely that we can quickly erase parental prejudice or recruit prejudiced parents to educate their offspring to tolerance.

But this pessimism ought not to apply to other agencies of socialization. The schools, the churches, and the mass media —the principal agencies of socialization outside the family—

may, as some of the authors have suggested, occasionally teach prejudice inadvertently. The ideal expectation, however, is that they will do just the opposite. The schools and the churches especially are expected to embody the highest values of the society and to assume a responsibility for inculcating them in the young.

Since an all-out effort has never been made, we do not know whether or not education for tolerance vigorously pursued among children can prevent the learning of prejudice. Neither do we know whether the schools, the churches, and the mass media, the institutions on which the nation would have to rely to furnish such education, could be motivated to work together to make the attempt. It would appear, nevertheless, that the nation's best chance to control prejudice lies in the educational leverage which these institutions have the capacity to supply.

It is unlikely that prejudice can be uprooted by any effort, no matter how intensive and long-term, directed to children alone. Adult prejudice constitutes too strong a counterforce to allow such ameliorative effort to be wholly successful. Therefore, in addition to more intensive effort to prevent the development of prejudice in the young, more effective means must be developed to challenge the prejudices of adults.

Once again, we have no precedent, no tested formula for action. Again, education—rather than some forced or semi-forced compliance to rules and laws—appears the most promising approach. Adults are less teachable than children, but still they can be taught both by precept and example. At the adult level, the churches and the mass media are probably in the best position to exert leverage because of the large adult audiences they reach. The schools, as they reach adults directly through adult education and indirectly through teaching their children, also have a role, though perhaps a lesser one. Other social institutions also have a potential contribution. In this book, we have singled out the business community for special attention, but labor unions, fraternal organizations, patriotic groups, social welfare agencies, and various arms of government—local, regional, and national—could also be recruited in the effort. Their assignment would not be to teach tolerance as would be expected of the schools, the mass media, and the churches but to illustrate by example that prejudiced attitudes and discriminatory behavior are indeed anathema to the American way of life. These institutions have the additional sanctions of laws and rules which can help reduce discrimination and provide members of diverse groups with the chance to work together and get to know each other.

Thus the greatest promise for the eventual control of prejudice and discrimination in America lies in a massive and sustained program of education carried on jointly by the major social institutions of the society. But how can so diverse a set of institutions possibly be persuaded to collaborate on such an ambitious venture? And, what precisely are they going to be asked to do? These questions must be faced if dream is to be moved toward reality. Before discussing them, however, we should remind ourselves of the existing situation, as described by our authors.

The Present Situation

What is immediately clear from the authors' descriptions of the state of each of the institutions is that the ideal we have been presenting in no way reflects present reality. The authors exhibit greater optimism about what the various institutions might do than about what they *are* doing. But no author anticipates a near miracle; on the other hand, no author would rule out making a significant try.

The schools, M. Brewster Smith tells us, pay lip service to the cause of tolerance but exert little effort and have little effect in instilling it in their charges. Schools are increasingly active, it is evident, in efforts to reduce discrimination and to eliminate the major deleterious effects of segregation. But such activity is rarely accompanied by a parallel effort to combat prejudice. As a result, children of different races are now interacting with each other in some cases—still a discouragingly low percentage—where they did not before. But, Smith reports, it is being left largely to the children on their own to figure out why they ought to interact. Often they do not figure it out. Smith cautions that the mere placing of black and white and brown children side by side in the classroom is not enough. He suggests that, in addition, creative programs of education for tolerance must be launched.

Obviously, the schools are far from performing as the ideal envisages. What are the possibilities? Charles Silberman, in his essay, is essentially equivocal in response to this question. Surely, he says, the schools can and ought to be doing considerably more to fight prejudice than they are doing now. He is skeptical, however, that the schools possess the leverage to effect change that many educators have attributed to them and that, indeed, the ideal assumes as well.

Rodney Stark and Charles Glock are at once optimistic and pessimistic in their evaluation of prejudice and the churches. They find, on the one hand, that the church is now more instrumental in promoting than in erasing prejudice. They see this, however, as largely an inadvertent byproduct of dogmas that are slowly losing their force. Consequently, they anticipate that in the natural course of events, the churches will upset the present balance. Moreover, they conceive that forces currently at work in the church (e.g., the increasing interest in Christian social ethics) might result in the cause of tolerance being given increasingly high priority among the church's tasks. They recognize that the church's power to effect change is limited, but they also point out that those most in need of change are those most likely to be found attending the churches. Hence, they constitute a reachable target group.

Dore Schary sees the mass media as exhibiting a genuine concern to help the cause of tolerance. He is considerably less sure that the media's performance measures up to their good intentions. Harnessing this good will to produce more effective performance is not conceived as impossible. But it means, Schary believes, that the media will have to become much more conscious of their assumptions about prejudice and the consequences which follow from them.

In assessing the business community's potential for effecting change, Howard Samuels is perhaps the most optimistic of the authors. He is also the most concrete in detailing where this potential lies. Samuels makes no assessment of the prospects for success, except to suggest that the world of work is an arena optimally suited to prejudice reduction. His chapter is primarily an urgent and persuasive plea to the business community to get on with the task.

Seymour Lipset paints a rather bleak portrait of the relation between politics and prejudice in America. In every era, he finds, there have been politicians who have used appeals to racial, religious, or ethnic prejudice to get votes, political parties that have adopted such appeals, and native-born political movements that have been weaned on them. He voices little hope that the picture will change drastically in the future. Yet he is careful to point out that the political arena has been the scene of most victories against prejudice in the past, and it is in the same arena, he suspects, that present victims of prejudice are most likely to win their struggle.

In sum, the authors uniformly agree that the institutions they examine can effect greater control of prejudice and discrimination than they now do. They also provide some specific insights into the nature and character of this capability, pointing out what each institution is doing and should be doing more of. Understandably, in light of their separate assignments, none of the authors outline a cross-institutional strategy for reducing the gap between promise and reality. This is the task to which we now turn.

The Prospects for Cross-institutional Efforts

We have sketchily looked at the ideal case of prejudice reduction and glanced back to note how far the institutions depart from this ideal. Now the question is what needs to be done pragmatically by these institutions, singly and collectively, to bring us closer to the ideal.

A first and obvious requirement is *commitment.* There must be created among the leaders of all major social institutions the conviction that the control of prejudice and discrimination is a legitimate and pressing institutional goal. As several authors have noted, lip service is given to the cause of tolerance, but in no institution, not even the churches, is combating prejudice given very high priority, and, in some institutions, it has no priority at all.

A second requirement, given the necessary commitment, is *planning for institutional action.* It is easy enough to declare that schools ought to educate for equality; that rules, regulations, and practices of business organizations should be nondiscriminatory; that the police should exemplify tolerance. But what specifically is to be taught, legislated, and regulated? Who is to formulate these courses of action? How are they to be carried out? Commitment is not enough unless it finds its outlet in a clear course of action.

Finally, developing and implementing blueprints for action takes *resources*—money, talent, and time. Nothing much is going to get done unless there is some way to pay for it. For all of the institutions we have been examining, even the wealthier ones, paying will be a problem no matter how high the motivation or how sophisticated the blueprints.

Even when the preliminary requirements are met, a whole host of problems will arise. How does one cope with bigoted parents who will not readily accept having their children learn that color does not matter? How does one retain commitment when success turns out to be slowly and painfully won? How does one overcome frustration when programs long in preparation end by failing? Confronting problems such as these will be a sign of progress, an indication at least that more basic requirements are being met and that *something* is being tried.

How exactly might the basic requirements—commitment, blueprints, and resources—be met for single institutions and for institutions working in consort?

Generating the institutional will to do something about prejudice is, in part, simply a matter of making the problems more salient. Widespread as they are, prejudice and discrimination are not generally highly visible. Their visibility has increased perhaps in recent times—especially since the long hot summers and the Kerner report. Mostly, however, the victims suffer in silence with little public recognition of how pervasive the problems are or how much hurt is being wrought.

One obvious way to make the problems more salient is to publicize the facts about prejudice and discrimination. But the facts are not readily available. We simply do not have comprehensive knowledge of how and to what extent Americans are prejudiced or about the distribution of prejudice in different social settings, in different parts of the country, and among different generations. Further, there is no periodic updating of what limited information we do have to permit realistic assessment of progress. Such information could mobilize a national concern about the social ills of prejudice and discrimination.

Greater public recognition does not automatically produce greater institutional activity, however. Institutional leaders must be convinced not only of the magnitude of these social problems but of their institutional responsibility to do something about them. This call to awareness and responsibility is a primary objective of this book, of the Berkeley symposium on prejudice which stimulated it, and indeed of the five-year research program on prejudice that led to the symposium. A number of the studies included in this long-range research were designed to evaluate institutional performance; they are represented in this volume by the chapters of Lipset, Smith, and Stark and Glock.

Widely enough disseminated, books and conferences and evaluative research can all contribute to overcoming institutional lethargy. But motivation, as we have suggested before, will not be enough. Institutions must not only want to do something but must also know what to do, and there is very little precedent for large-scale institutional campaigns against prejudice. The development and testing of such programs are a first order of business if we are to move beyond merely talking about prejudice. We know generally, of course, what institutions ought to try to do. Some suggestions have been sketched in this book. Painstaking action-oriented research must be tried; prescriptions must be carried out on a pilot scale, evaluated, widely applied when they are found workable, modified and retested when they are not. Moreover, the attack must be a coordinated one, not a piecemeal and chaotic effort by each school district, parish church, or newspaper acting on its own.

Until this investment to build and test model programs has been made, one can only speculate about what might emerge as the best strategy for each institution to adopt and how they might best work together to effect change. So, for example, the schools could conceivably be restructured along the lines Charles Silberman has suggested so that they would teach tolerance by virtue of the basic ways they were organized and operated. To put such a massive reorganization into practice would obviously not be easy. Perhaps it can be tested first on small scale. Perhaps, despite Silberman's skepticism, a large part of the burden of change can be effected by instruction—e.g., special devices designed to teach children what prejudice and discrimination are all about. Conceivably, nothing now envisioned will be found to work, and it will be necessary to start again in rethinking and implementing the role of the schools in prejudice reduction.

As for the churches, their greatest contribution, as Rodney Stark and Charles Glock suggest, could well lie in a reformulation of the way doctrine is taught. This is probably not the only way, however, that the churches can help. It would seem, offhand, that they can be efficacious also by teaching more vigorously that prejudice is a sin. All might do what some churches are already doing—revise their Sunday-school curriculum material to give more explicit attention to the problems of prejudice and discrimination, or devote their entire adult education program over an extended period of time to an explanation of the roots of prejudice. Perhaps some combination of these and still-to-be-invented means will be required.

The mass media, as Dore Schary points out, can clearly do more to control prejudice both in their treatment of news and in what they do to entertain. The question is how to do this. The media have proposed and received a host of suggestions that range from increasing the amount of positive human interest news coverage about minority groups to highlighting prejudice and discrimination as the themes of dramatic presentations. While they have tried some of the ideas piecemeal, the media have never addressed themselves to the difficult task of scrutinizing the possibilities carefully and subjecting the best ones to pilot programs and experimentation to learn what can be tried and what will bring results.

Inventing programs to try may be easier for institutions whose capability for exerting leverage comes through example and practice rather than through formal or informal instruction. We are thinking of industry, labor, the police, the courts, social welfare organizations, social clubs, and patriotic groups. In the formulation of their internal rules and regulations these institutions are in a position to manifest their commitment to tolerance in practice. Howard Samuels, in his essay on industry and prejudice, illustrates the possibilities succinctly and well. Indeed, the beginning strategy he sets forth for industry to try provides a model which with minor modifications would be applicable to other institutions as well.

Strategies such as the one proposed by Mr. Samuels need to be pretested before they are widely adopted. They are not likely to be effective if the rules and regulations are not enforced, of course. But even when they are enforced, pay-off is not automatic. They may have the desired effect or they may boomerang.

The possibility of sheer ineffectiveness or even of boomerang is a danger, of course, with all ameliorative action. Consequently, the constant need for hard evaluative research cannot be underscored too strongly. Without knowing what works and what does not and why, we will rarely through good will alone be lucky enough to make the right decisions about where to invest energy, money, and time.

Thus far, we have remarked primarily on the need for workable intra-institutional strategies that can become models for wide adoption. Interinstitutional collaboration also must be explored. It would be most desirable and natural to have a partnership for prejudice reduction in which industry cooperates with labor, the police work with the courts, and the media of all kinds work together. Another logical possibility is collaboration between schools and industry or labor on adult education programs. The mass media could easily work with schools and churches in the development of audio-visual educational materials.

Following through on any of these suggestions for program development will be expensive. Preparing school curriculum materials, developing specialized parish education programs, creating a television series—these are major undertakings requiring considerable time and talent on the part of well-paid professionals. Testing the effectiveness of such programs—a hitherto almost unexplored field—will add to the cost. And, once tested programs are ready, materials will have to be paid for, distribution will have to be arranged, and people will have to be trained to use the materials.

Where are the funds to come from? Mostly they will have to come from the institutions themselves. Seed money to get started might be available to some institutions from private foundations, and the schools might find it possible to generate subsidies from the federal government. Foundation and government sources might also be tapped to help pay for research designed to evaluate programs as they are developed. Such sources altogether, however, can be expected to provide only a fraction of what will be required.

To suggest that the institutions themselves would have to bear the cost would appear, at first glance, to make wholly utopian all that we have been saying. Schools everywhere are operating under tight budgets. The churches are more financially strapped than they have been in decades. The budgets of government agencies are being trimmed. Despite their large profit margins, the mass media and industry do not regard themselves as eleemosynary institutions with funds to invest in possibly controversial programs that do not promise a direct financial return.

These shortages are obstacles, but in the end they are not likely to prove the crucial ones. At this juncture, clearly, it is failure of institutional will and know-how rather than any dearth of institutional resources that prevents prejudice and discrimination from being fought more effectively. If and when institutions want to do something badly enough, and know how to do it, the financial problems will not loom nearly so large as they do when contemplating the possibilities in the abstract.

What is missing in the real world and in our own proposals still is any assignment of responsibility for guiding and overseeing the nation's efforts to control prejudice and discrimination. Central coordinating agencies have been crucial to the progress that the nation has made in the control of physical disease; one thinks of the highly successful National Foundation for Infantile Paralysis as one spectacular example of the results of coordinated planning. What we need now is a National Foundation against Prejudice and Discrimination, our most virulent social disease.

Such an agency could perform a variety of important functions. It could take the lead in promoting the regular collection of data on incidence and could even become the collection agency. It could also be assigned responsibility for publicizing the results of such data collection efforts and more generally for keeping the public informed about how much prejudice and discrimination exists, about the forms that they take, about their causes, and about the success of efforts to combat them.

The agency could play a pump-priming role. It could make available a staff of qualified creative and research personnel who could help institutions or could themselves develop and test pilot programs. Such an agency could also encourage counterpart agencies to direct and coordinate activities within particular institutions as a remedy for the present dispersion of effort. As institutions come to bear more of the burden themselves, the central agency might become increasingly a coordinating body.

In the distant future, such an agency might become an arm of the federal government, perhaps a special division of the Department of Health, Education, and Welfare. For the moment, however, it is most likely to come into being as a private organization. To maximize its effectiveness such an agency should be created and jointly supported by the institutions it is intended to work with and serve—for example, the National Education Association, the National Association of Manufacturers, the AFL-CIO, the National Council of Churches, the National Catholic Social Welfare Conference, the Synagogue Council of America, the National Association of Broadcasters, and the American Newspaper and Periodical Publishers Associations. Cooperative support of the agency by these institutions cannot realistically be expected without a good deal of prior work by an intensely interested group. If such an agency is to come into being sooner rather than later, one or more private foundations will probably have to provide the stimulus and the initial seed money. No one agency would have the leverage to accomplish everything to which the nation, in principle, aspires. But it would take us a long way on the road to equality for all Americans.

There is, of course, a degree of wishful thinking in all that we have said. Institutional effort probably cannot be mustered to move as far or as fast as we have proposed, even though these proposals are fairly modest and evolutionary compared to the current battle cries of the far right and the far left. Both the fact-finding and the program-producing part of the job are likely to have to battle public apathy. And without public pressure, institutions will probably not heed this or any other call to their unfinished business. It is thus very possible that the response to prejudice will continue to be determined mostly by the power of the victims to protest it.

This would be most unfortunate. For, as we have noted repeatedly, these are no ordinary times for America. Minority groups numbering close to 40 million Americans, long the quiet victims of prejudice and discrimination, are no longer of a mind to remain quiet. They want change, and they want it quickly. Many of them believe that no evolutionary reform within the system will do the job. And the majority does not seem to have the understanding or the will to respond warmly, generously, and effectively. Instead the course of events is likely to be determined by the fear and bigotry that our nation has allowed to simmer too long. There are already signs of friendlier public reception to extremist solutions both of the left and the right. It may even now be too late to repair the damages. Given the revolutionary temper of our times, our institutions' collective ability to deal with prejudice may well spell the difference between their viability and their defeat. But before we talk of scrapping these institutions we must give them every possible chance to help heal the cleavages in our national life. For the sake of principle and, indeed, of survival, men of good will must make this a better, more humane America.

C.Y.G.

E.S.

HOW IT LOOKS FROM THE CENTER OF THE CITY[1]

RICHARD HATCHER

Urban America is wallowing in decay and despair. The ghetto does not recede but proliferates outward at an alarming geometric rate, engulfing then mangling the wretched of the earth. The black man is denied acquisition of skills in a technology which has no use for the unskilled. The public school is a segregated detention center where the valedictorian requires remedial reading. Our waterways are septic tanks; the very air we breathe is carcinogenic. The density of the city is matched only by its ugliness. What is old is often forlorn. What is new is rarely imaginative. In a society where the balance sheet is the bible, the cost accountant has become the architect.

We live in a state of self-imposed isolation, insensitive to the distress of others. In the borough of Queens, a woman is brutally murdered while dozens of apartment-dwellers listen to her screams without lifting a finger to help her. When the nation's press reports that 45 per cent of all black people are

---

[1] The book's last chapter, like its first, is devoted to a call to conscience by black Americans. Here, Richard Hatcher, the first Negro to be elected Mayor of Gary, Indiana, tells how he sees it from the inner city. His purposes, of course, are to champion a cause and to further it. These are the things this book seeks to do. Only time will tell whether it will succeed. (The editors)

impoverished, the American conscience is not pricked: there is no national revulsion, only terrifying silence.

Imaginative programs such as Headstart, Model Cities, Rent Subsidies, and OEO are either totally unfunded or almost starved to death. Our government and society have chosen to spend $73 billion annually for gunpowder, but only pennies for people. Whatever the priority of values to which our government adheres one conclusion is inescapable: black people and poor people do not come first.

The few small efforts that government makes to alleviate the suffering of poor people in this country are usually crisis-oriented and temporary. A year after the Kerner Commission report, we were no better off. We were probably worse off.

The racial crisis of our cities is a confluence of two distinct, yet related forces. The first is relentless racism, altered during its 300-year history only in its style, not its content. The second vector is a rampaging and unchecked urban decay.

Employment laws bare the sinews of racism. A few statistics amply tell the story. In 1948, 7.6 per cent of Negro males in our country were unemployed. This jumped to 22.6 per cent in 1965. Out of 970,000 new jobs created in the decade from 1955 to 1965, only 36,000 went to Negro youth. Percentage-wise, twice as many black as white adults are unemployed. Unemployment rates are higher for nonwhite high school graduates than for white high school dropouts. The median income for a Negro college graduate is only $5,020; that is $110 less than the earnings of white male high school dropouts. A black man must have between one and three years of college before he can expect to earn as much as a white man with less than eight years of school. Furthermore, after completing college and spending at least one year in graduate school, a black man can expect to earn only as much as a white man who only finished high school. A white high school graduate may expect to earn $253,000 during his lifetime, while a Negro with five or more years of college may expect to earn only $246,000. The horrifying truth implied by such statistics is that the people of the ghetto have been forced to undergo a savage suppression of the human spirit, the mangling of dignity, a lifetime of humiliation.

Resistance and Black Power

The Negro ghetto has only two possible responses to its wretchedness: resignation or resistance. Resistance assumes many forms. Whatever white fear was generated by Detroit's rebellious expression of black power may very well have been matched by Gary's white hostility to the more benign politicized form of black power in the form of my mayoral campaign. With only a couple of exceptions, no major local white political Democratic Party figure came to our support. My own county chairman was less than kind in his frequent references to my candidacy. In effect I ended up being opposed by both local political parties.

In a city overwhelmingly Democratic, approximately 17 per cent of the white voters cast their vote for me, and we won the election by a narrow margin of approximately 1,800 votes —hardly a landslide. The day after election, *The Gary Post-Tribune* pointed out in a front-page editorial what a fine white vote we received and what an immense debt we owed the white citizens. The most tragic element of our racist society is that it cannot recognize its own racism. For decades, 95 per cent of Gary's huge Negro vote had carried one white Democratic mayoral candidate after another into office. There were no editorials then. No savants then suggested that the mayor-elect owed any obligations to the black voters, those who led lives of quiet desperation and who had pinned their last waning hopes on the winning candidate; no suggestion was made then by the comfortable good samaritans that the mayor-elect owed to Negroes, either out of a sense of Christian morality or political debt, any obligation whatsoever. No! Obligations were never felt or asserted, and therefore quite expectably, none were fulfilled. With some degree of recklessness, however, I submit that Negroes, ancient victims of exploitation and neglect, hence highly sensitized to it, need not be told of their debts and obligations to their white brothers and sisters. They are committed to a multiracial society. And we shall not simply talk about it; we shall live it.

Lest this picture of the Gary election appear excessively bleak, let me add that there were many white persons who worked in the campaign with the devotion of the early disciples. They were lonely and isolated, but they never complained. Some were threatened and their noses were literally bloodied, but they did not flinch. They slept few hours and wore out the soles of their shoes, impervious to insult and defamation. It is neither maudlin nor apocryphal to say that the mutual love and respect that developed between the black and white workers during the campaign—the mission that brought them together and the bond that held them together —will never be torn asunder. It was an exciting glimpse into what a future society can really bring forth, if it has the will to do so.

But the experiment in Gary, like other such experiments, cannot succeed without a metamorphosis in American institutional life. We must insist on a national renaissance where people, freedom, and culture take precedence over bricks, guns, and profits. We must return to those values that are the very foundation of our society; we must devote substantial resources to tasks that cry out to be done and that in performance would reduce significantly the gaps between the poor and the well-off, the black and the white; we must engage our energies, our imaginations, and our efforts to move toward a national community of interest and action, so that the system that has worked so well for most Americans does not continue to fail the poor and the black.

Whether in national or local crisis, time and time again the American people have been required to abandon narrow self-interest to do what was required of them. When they understood what was at stake, when they could identify with the need of other human beings or with broader self-interests, they have done what had to be done. The question today is whether we are prepared to meet headlong and in a meaningful way the problems that threaten to destroy and tear asunder the very fabric of our country. I am convinced that there will be no quiet summers in our cities unless massive federal money is allocated to provide the jobs, the housing, the schools and welfare programs for those contained within the walls of the ghettos.

What would it cost to launch an imaginative, effective federal program to transform the ghetto? The "freedom budget" outlined by the A. Philip Randolph Institute calls for $185 billion to be spent over the next ten years. Professor Seymour Melman of Columbia University places the requirement at $20 billion a year.

We now spend billions for armaments and only millions for housing, schools, and social services. The Ninetieth Congress, committed to a huge arms budget, was unable or unwilling to find the funds for human needs. There were not many at the Washington Urban Conference who applauded New York's Mayor Lindsay when he said: "If our defense commitment is blocking a vigorous effort to end those agonies in the slums, the commitment should be reassessed." Dr. Martin Luther King used to tell us that our government spent $300,000 to kill one Viet-Cong and only $50 on each poor person in this country. A searching reassessment may well cause us to reverse our national priorities.

The Negro and American Institutions

"I hear it was charged against me that I sought to destroy institutions, but really, I am neither for nor against institutions." So wrote Walt Whitman many years ago, and so it is with American Negroes today, who see themselves the victims of institutional doublethink. When Governor Wallace stands in the doorway of the University of Alabama to keep a black student from entering, he claims to be preserving the sacred institution of the state university. When a city like Gary passes an open-occupancy ordinance, real estate brokers and white homeowners oppose it on the grounds that self-seeking Negroes aim to pervert the institution of private property. When Negro workers go to court, or to the picket line, not against an employer but against a union which keeps them from gaining membership, they are accused of seeking to abrogate the free trade union movement. When we kneel-in or pray-in on the steps of a Southern church, we are attacking the institution of religion. When we come to a local minister or priest or rabbi to support us in some endeavor which may make his parishioners uncomfortable or even angry, then we are attacking the church as an institution. So it should not be surprising that, like Whitman, I am neither for nor against institutions in themselves. Rather, I am concerned with their teachings and their practices.

The fact is that the institutions so hallowed by American tradition have left the Negro outside the door. Furthermore, many of these institutions have kept him quiescent and passive because they have helped to foster the illusion that, if he only "acts nicely," the institutions of godly men will in time triumph and help him find his place in American life.

I should like to share some of my personal experiences with the institutions of my own city. In Gary, I confronted anew the dreadful fact that even the capable leaders of well-intentioned institutions, such as the labor movement, apparently cannot bring their people with them. So for example, the District Director of the United Steel Workers of America supported my candidacy as he has traditionally supported the candidacy of the Democratic nominee for mayor. He spoke in my behalf and contributed generously to my campaign. But he was not able to lead more than the merest handful of his white membership to the polls to cast the traditional Democratic vote—because this time the Democrat was black.

This is a shocking fact. Such fine Negro leaders as A. Philip Randolph, himself a vice-president of the AFL-CIO, have believed that the trade union movement, the great liberal hope of the 1930's, would in time come to the aid of the black community, would be that much-vaunted white ally for freedom. Indeed, some black men have given their lives for this very trade union movement in that belief. Yet ironically many of those who were most bitterly opposed to my candidacy were steel workers, and "good" union men.

And what of the church? I am a Baptist by upbringing. Of a Sunday morning you will find me in the House of God with my neighbors. But on Sunday afternoon, I look at my TV screen and I see Catholic nuns, sweetfaced, with the haunting eyes of the ancient martyrs, being clubbed to the ground by members of their own church because they are marching in behalf of open housing. I see a priest in Milwaukee vilified by other priests, cursed by his parishioners, because he leads angry young blacks in marches for an open-occupancy law. In my own city, I am forced to acknowledge that some of the worst racist poison has been injected by members of that great and centuries-old institution the Catholic Church. A few courageous white clergymen spoke out against blatant racist vote-stealing and stood watch on election day, but they were only a few and they were able to bring only a few of their flock with them. The white Protestant and Jewish communities also built their part of the mountain of hate meant as a grave for black hope.

I report these inequities not to traduce the church or to attack the labor movement, but to show why black Americans echo Walt Whitman. Negroes have very little concern with institutions in and of themselves but a great deal of concern with what these institutions do in terms of full democracy, full equality. I am reminded of Amos in the Bible, the great preacher of social justice whose words to an Israel riddled by oppression and injustice might well be echoed by all non-white Americans today:

> I hate, I despise your feast, and I take no delight in your solemn-assemblies. Even though you offer me your burnt-offerings. . . . I will not accept them: and the peace offerings of your fatted beasts, I will not look upon. Take away from me the noise of your songs: to the melody of your harps I will not listen. But let *justice* roll down like waters, and *righteousness* like an over-flowing stream. [Amos 5:21–24]

Amos tells us further that God is not satisfied with worship that denies the rights of any human being. When it becomes irrelevant to human needs, what is done inside the temple has little value. For Amos says that our God is more concerned with what is right than he is with rites performed within the temple walls.

Black Americans agree: the espousal of great ideas is simply no longer enough. Great institutions must become effective social forces for the fulfillment of such great ideas. We suffer with the clubbed nun, with the courageous priest, with the minister run over by the bulldozer, with the rabbi threatened with death. But we cannot really trust their institutions as such, until their members join their leaders. When the citizens of Gage Park, Watts, Berkeley, and Gary are ready to follow their leaders and throw wide the gate, then, and only then, can we trust the institutions of which I speak. That is the great task which faces white America.

This is the task not only of church and labor union, but of every institution in American life. The schools have failed and so have the universities—witness the Negro dropout rate. Large business concerns have put some of our pretty women in their front offices while they have kept us mostly out of their shops and totally off their boards of directors. Look at any of the institutions of which Americans are so proud and there you will see a black hiatus—an empty place where for 300 years Negroes should have been. They are now determined to be there at all costs.

In this determination, I believe, lies the ultimate importance of my election, and the election of other Negroes to high political office. For by the very fact that we seek political office, we say to you that we have not given up hope for the greatest of our institutions, the democratic political process. We will bend every effort to make this institution work. We will run our offices with every good intention and make every effort to do a good job for all men—but only the white majority in America can make democracy work in full. If white Americans have the strength to give these democratic institutions vitality, to give blacks within their framework the rightful place they should have had three centuries ago, the nation will survive.

It is a nip-and-tuck battle, this battle for survival. If democracy can really function, then we shall, perhaps, see the day when Walt Whitman's conception of the nation will come true, for the poet who had no special love for institutions had profound feeling for the brotherhood of man:

> I will plant companionship thick as trees along the rivers
> of America,

And along the shores of the great lakes, and all over the
    prairies,
I will make inseparable cities with their arms about each
    other's necks,
By the love of comrades,
By the manly love of comrades.

The elections in Gary and Cleveland represent a new plateau of political maturity for America, a serious setback for
backlash and back stab. For this we are all grateful. But with
this new plateau comes the realization that it was a new
Negro who reached it. This new Negro rejects the concept
of gradualism; first, because he has learned by cruel experience that gradualism means never and, second, because freedom is not a gift to be parceled out in bits and pieces. Freedom
is a birthright. Every American citizen is entitled to it. It
belongs to him. Not next year, not next week, not tomorrow,
but *now*.

Each of us, somewhere in the deep recesses of his being, is
haunted by a dream. For many of us, the dream is all that
keeps us going. It is a dream that someday, somehow, working together, we can effect change, that together we can build
a new world, that together we can build those "inseparable
cities with their arms about each other's necks."

A fresh breeze is blowing. It invigorates us all. For the first
time in ages, people dare to hope. They know that the heavens
have not willed that our cities be mired in corruption, that
children be bitten by rats, or that black and white be pitted
against each other.

The people know that it can and must be different, that the
ugliness of slums can be made to disappear and beauty to take
its place. They know that all of us can learn to work, play,
live, and pray side by side, that government need not destroy
the human spirit but can rekindle it so that little children

will know the smell not of garbage rotting, but of flowers blooming. Today's ghetto child shall be tomorrow's poet.

The voices crying out from the ghettos of our country will not be stilled by more suppressive measures. They will not be stilled by more antiriot laws. They will only be stilled by profound changes in our current social order. We need leadership at every level of government that will rally the people to bring about these changes.

We may have lost our way, but I believe we are groping toward the light in America and will find it if we all work together. There is a famous statement in black folklore:

> We ain't what we ought to be.
> We ain't what we gonna be.
> We ain't what we wanta be.
> But, thank God,
> We ain't what we was.

ABOUT THE CONTRIBUTORS

CHARLES Y. GLOCK is Professor of Sociology and Research Sociologist, Survey Research Center, University of California, Berkeley.

RICHARD HATCHER is Mayor of Gary, Indiana.

THEODORE M. HESBURGH is President, Notre Dame University, and Chairman of the U.S. Civil Rights Commission.

SEYMOUR MARTIN LIPSET is Professor of Government and Social Relations, Harvard University.

SAUNDERS REDDING is an author and educator and Director of Research and Publication, National Endowment for the Humanities.

HOWARD J. SAMUELS is former Administrator, Small Business Administration.

DORE SCHARY, playwright and producer, is National Chairman of the Anti-Defamation League of B'nai B'rith.

ELLEN SIEGELMAN is an Assistant Research Psychologist in the Psychology Department, University of California, Berkeley.

CHARLES E. SILBERMAN is the Director of the Carnegie Study for the Education of Educators.

M. BREWSTER SMITH is Professor and Chairman, Department of Psychology, University of Chicago.